NICE MOOD CARD

WILD THING MOOD CARD/YEAR-ROUND CLASSROOM GUIDANCE GAMES
© 2007 MAR*CO PRODUCTS, INC. 1-800-448-2197

MEAN MOOD CARD

WILD THING MOOD CARD/YEAR-ROUND CLASSROOM GUIDANCE GAMES
© 2007 MAR*CO PRODUCTS, INC. 1-800-448-2197

D1710345

FOR GRADES
K-5

YEAR-ROUND
CLASSROOM GUIDANCE GAMES

MONTHLY GAMES, LESSONS, AND ACTIVITIES
FOR CLASSROOMS AND SMALL GROUPS

By
Marianne Vandawalker

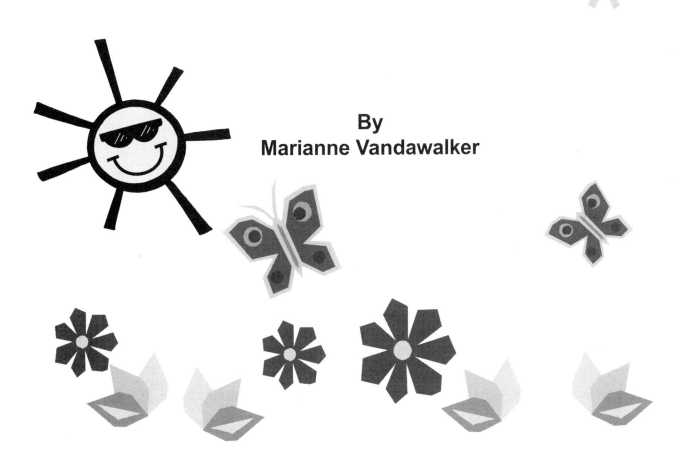

YEAR-ROUND CLASSROOM GUIDANCE GAMES

GRAPHIC DESIGN: Cameon Funk

10-DIGIT ISBN: 1-57543-149-1   13-DIGIT ISBN: 978-1-57543-149-9

COPYRIGHT © 2007 MAR*CO PRODUCTS, INC.
    Published by mar*co products, inc.
    1443 Old York Road
    Warminster, PA 18974
    1-800-448-2197
    www.marcoproducts.com

PRINTED IN THE U.S.A.

TABLE OF CONTENTS

INTRODUCTION

Guidance activities can be integrated with other school programs, and *Year-Round Classroom Guidance Games* is a tool to help relate the guidance program to classroom activities. When counselors sprinkle guidance-related topics with seasonal themes like snowflakes, flowers, or leaves, students relate guidance lessons to the total curriculum.

Year-Round Classroom Guidance Games includes lessons on the primary counseling issues that need to be presented and practiced in the general school population. The book also provides in-depth exercises for small-group counseling.

In the elementary setting, bulletin boards, math, spelling, writing, reading, and even field trips may be centered on the season or holiday. This book offers guidance lessons related to seasonal themes and includes lessons on:

- Social Skills
- Good Character
- Manners
- Study Skills & Goal Setting
- Responsible Decisions
- Friendship
- Conflict Resolution
- Listening
- Patriotism
- Remembrance & Respect

Although this book associates lessons with certain holidays/months, some lessons, such as *Some Like It Hot* (anger management), may be presented at any time of the year. *Majesty's Manners* give students an opportunity to practice good social skills, an ongoing necessity for young people as they continue to develop and change. In *I Spy*, students practice listening, a skill classroom teachers will appreciate your help in developing. *Wild Thing's Choice* teaches students how to make good decisions, helping guide them through a successful school year. *In And Out Of The Corn Maze* and *Let's Stick Together* teach students to develop friendship skills, an important part of getting along with others and preparing to meet life's challenges.

Simplicity is another important element of the lessons included in *Year-Round Classroom Guidance Games.* A counselor often has limited space in which to present his/her lessons, and limited time in which to make an impact. The involvement games in this book can be used in both small or large settings and require few props. The lessons require minimal preparation.

These activities will meet with the instant approval of both students and instructors. *Year-Round Classroom Guidance Games* provides students with relevant high-interest, high-impact experiences. When you announce a pizza party you will immediately command students' attention. If you show some of the simple props, such as a bottle of bubbles or a flashlight, you will pique students' interest. When you add a bit of competition, students must listen more closely.

Enjoy *Year-Round Classroom Guidance Games.* Gain confidence in your lessons, connect with students as well as teachers, and make a real difference in today's educational world.

INSTRUCTIONS FOR USING THE CD

The CD found on the inside back cover provides ADOBE® PDF files. The 10-per-page cards are designed to be printed on paper, cardstock, or Avery® #5871 white clean edge business cards. (Please note: Due to differences in the tolerances/settings of printers, the printout of the business card template version may not line up properly. If you have problems using this version, you may need to change your printer's settings. If the problem can not be resolved, please use one of the other provided pages to produce the gamecards.)

System requirements to open PDF (.pdf) files:
Adobe Reader® 5.0 or newer (compatible with Windows 2000® or newer or Mac OS 9.0® or newer).

These files offer the user color and black and white versions of the reproducible pages found in the book. For example: *016_yearroundguid.pdf* is the same as page 16 in the book.

Each PDF file may include one or more versions of the page (color, Avery® business card template, and/or grayscale/black and white versions.)

These files cannot be modified/edited.

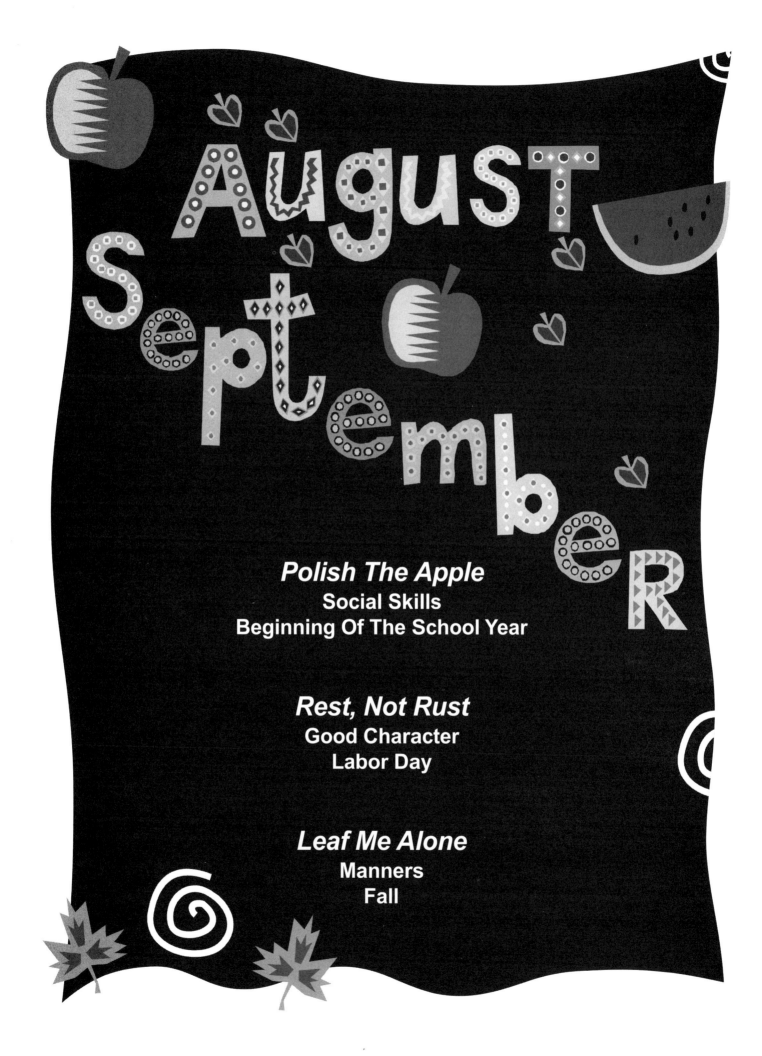

AUGUST

September

Polish The Apple
Social Skills
Beginning Of The School Year

Rest, Not Rust
Good Character
Labor Day

Leaf Me Alone
Manners
Fall

POLISH THE APPLE
Social Skills/Beginning Of The School Year/Grades K-3

PURPOSE:

To help students learn to accept authority

OBJECTIVE:

To win points for your team by displaying the correct response more quickly than the other team

MATERIALS NEEDED:

For each student:
    None

For the leader:
- ☐ Apple Cards (page 16)
- ☐ Cardstock or paper
- ☐ 4 paper plates
- ☐ 4 rulers or paint sticks
- ☐ Marker
- ☐ Tape or stapler and staples
- ☐ Scissors

GAME PREPARATION:

On one side of each paper plate, write the words *Yes, Ma'am/Yes, Sir* and draw a smiling face. On the other side of each paper plate, write the words *No, Ma'am/No, Sir* and draw a frowning face. Tape or staple each paper plate to the end of a ruler/paint stick. Reproduce one or more copies of the Apple Cards on paper or cardstock and cut the cards apart. Laminate the cards for durability (optional). (*Note:* The number of Apple Cards you will need depends on the number of students playing the game and the number of demand/requests you will read to each group.)

PROCEDURE:

▸ Ask the students:

> **Who is in authority or in charge at home?** (parents, older siblings, relatives, etc.) **At school?** (teachers, principal, etc.) **In the community?** (police officers, community leaders, etc.)
>
> **What are some things that adults in charge might ask you to do?** (chores, homework, obey rules, etc.)

▸ Divide the class into two teams. (Girls versus boys, one side of the room versus the other, etc.)

▸ Choose two players from each team to come to the front of the room. Give each of the players a paper plate.

▸ Tell the group:

> *I will call out something that an adult, such as your parent or teacher, might ask you to do. If you are one of students representing your team, turn your paper plate to indicate the best response to my request or demand, then quickly hold it up in front of your face. The team whose two members show the best response most quickly will receive one point. For example, if I say, "Stop talking in class," you will turn the paper plate to the smiling face to show the best response to that request as being* Yes Ma'am/Yes Sir. *If you show the correct face and put the plate in front of your face more quickly than the other team, your team wins an Apple Card. Each Apple Card is worth one point.*

▸ Decide, based on the number of students in the class, how many requests to read to each group of four players. Make sure each student gets a turn to play. After you have read the selected number of requests, choose new players from each team. Begin the game and play for as long as time allows. When the allotted time has elapsed, declare a winner.

▸ Authority Requests (* marks the *No, Ma'am/No, Sir* answers)

      Pick up the toys on the floor.
      Pick up the trash on the floor.
      Stop talking.
      Line up for lunch.
*   Do you want to cause trouble?
*   Did you yell at me? (This could be either a *yes* or *no* answer.)
      Finish your homework.
      Turn off the TV.
      Don't hold onto the ball.

* Did you get into trouble today?
  Don't call out.
  Stand up.
  Sit down.
* Are you going to fuss?
* Do you want your name on the board for bad behavior?
  Turn in your test.
* Are you looking at his paper to see his answers?
  You can't have candy at the store.
  You can't yell at me.
  Your friend can't come over to play today.
* Did you make this mess? (This could be either a *yes* or *no* answer.)
  Listen to me.
  Wait a minute.
  Let me help you.
  Come away from there.
* Are you sure that's what happened? (This could be either a *yes* or *no* answer.)
* Are you looking for trouble?

CONCLUSION:

▸ Ask the students the following questions:

When is it easy to agree to do what someone in charge asks you to do?

When is it difficult to agree to do what someone in charge asks you to do?

How do you feel when you follow directions from the adult who is in charge? Why do you feel that way?

APPLE CARD/YEAR-ROUND CLASSROOM GUIDANCE GAMES
© 2007 MAR•CO PRODUCTS, INC. 1-800-448-2197

APPLE CARD/YEAR-ROUND CLASSROOM GUIDANCE GAMES
© 2007 MAR•CO PRODUCTS, INC. 1-800-448-2197

APPLE CARD/YEAR-ROUND CLASSROOM GUIDANCE GAMES
© 2007 MAR•CO PRODUCTS, INC. 1-800-448-2197

APPLE CARD/YEAR-ROUND CLASSROOM GUIDANCE GAMES
© 2007 MAR•CO PRODUCTS, INC. 1-800-448-2197

APPLE CARD/YEAR-ROUND CLASSROOM GUIDANCE GAMES
© 2007 MAR•CO PRODUCTS, INC. 1-800-448-2197

APPLE CARD/YEAR-ROUND CLASSROOM GUIDANCE GAMES
© 2007 MAR•CO PRODUCTS, INC. 1-800-448-2197

APPLE CARD/YEAR-ROUND CLASSROOM GUIDANCE GAMES
© 2007 MAR•CO PRODUCTS, INC. 1-800-448-2197

APPLE CARD/YEAR-ROUND CLASSROOM GUIDANCE GAMES
© 2007 MAR•CO PRODUCTS, INC. 1-800-448-2197

APPLE CARD/YEAR-ROUND CLASSROOM GUIDANCE GAMES
© 2007 MAR•CO PRODUCTS, INC. 1-800-448-2197

APPLE CARD/YEAR-ROUND CLASSROOM GUIDANCE GAMES
© 2007 MAR•CO PRODUCTS, INC. 1-800-448-2197

REST, NOT RUST
Good Character/Labor Day/Grades 2-5

PURPOSE:

To help students understand how much effort hard work involves

OBJECTIVE:

To help students visualize themselves in a working situation and realize how refreshed they feel after resting

MATERIALS NEEDED:

For each student:
- ☐ Piece of drawing paper
- ☐ Pencil

For the leader:
- ☐ Chalkboard and chalk

GAME PREPARATION:

Gather the necessary materials.

PROCEDURE:

▸ Ask the students:

What are some kinds of work that your parents do? (Accept the names of jobs as well as specific tasks their parents may perform.)

What do your parents like to do after they have worked very hard? (Go fishing, watch TV, go for a walk, play sports, etc.)

What do you see and hear that makes you know your parents have worked hard? (They may say they have worked hard, explain what they did that day, yawn, want to lie down or go to bed early, etc.)

What kind of work do you do? (Chores, different activities at school, etc.)

How do you feel after doing that work? (Tired, need to stop and rest, proud of what was accomplished, etc.)

▸ Distribute a piece of drawing paper to each student. Make sure each student has a pencil. Then say:

Fold your paper lengthwise by bringing the left side of the paper to the right side of the paper.

Open up your paper.

At the top of the left-hand side, write the word WORK in large letters.

At the top of the right-hand side, write the word REST in large letters.

Under the word WORK, draw a picture of yourself performing an activity such as the one you just shared with the group. Make your picture large enough to be seen all of the way in the back of the classroom.

Under the word REST, draw a picture of how you feel or what you do after working hard.

▸ Have the students share their pictures with the group.

CONCLUSION:

▸ Write the word *REST* on the chalkboard. Then say:

If I change one letter in REST by erasing the E and putting a U in its place, what word do I have? (Erase the E and put a U in its place. Have the students look at the word *RUST.*)

What is the difference between people who REST and people who RUST? (After working and taking a rest, people have two choices. They can go back to work and make something out of their lives. Or they can RUST by staying in one place, not working, and not accomplishing very much.)

▸ Read the following scenario, then have the students answer the questions:

A person whose test paper is returned sees that he or she marked wrong answers for several questions. This person worked while taking the test, then rested until the graded paper was returned. What would the person who is RESTING do after getting the paper back? What would the person who is RUSTING do after getting the paper back? (The person who is resting would find out the correct answers to the ones he/she answered incorrectly. The person who is rusting would ignore the wrong answers and throw the paper away.

▸ If time permits, have the students give other examples.

LEAF ME ALONE
Manners/Fall/Grades 1-5

PURPOSE:

To allow the students to practice good manners by sharing

OBJECTIVE:

To accumulate more same-color leaves than the other group

MATERIALS NEEDED:

For each student group:
  None

For the leader:
- ☐ Leaves (page 22)
- ☐ Scissors
- ☐ Large paper bag
- ☐ 6 small paper bags
- ☐ 6 different colors of construction paper or cardstock

GAME PREPARATION:

Reproduce a large number of Leaves on six different colors of construction paper or cardstock. Cut out the leaves and put them in the large paper bag. Randomly choose six leaves from the large bag and put them in a small paper bag. Do this for each of the six small paper bags.

PROCEDURE:

▸ Ask the students to give examples of good manners.

▸ Divide the class into six groups. Give each group a small paper bag containing six colored leaves.

▸ Tell the students:

Do not take the leaves out of your group's bag, and don't let the other groups know the colors of the leaves in your group's bag.

Decide, as a group, what color leaves you want to begin saving. Then your group may ask any other group for the color of the leaves you have decided to save. Do this by walking over to another group and asking, "May we have all of your (color) leaves?" If the group has any leaves of the color you requested, they will say, "Yes, we'll share with you." If that group does not have any leaves that color, they will say, "We can't help you."

Pay attention to what color leaves each group wants to save. If you have that leaf color in your group's bag and the group did not ask your group for it, you may ask for the color and take that group's leaves.

The changing supply of leaves in your small bag may make it necessary for your group save leaves of a different color than you originally wanted to save.

When you share your leaves by giving them to another group, you may refill your bag by picking, from the large bag, as many leaves as you shared. When doing this, you must carefully transfer the leaves from the large bag to your small bag without looking at the leaves and without letting the other groups see the color of the leaves. (Note: For some groups, the leader may want to hand out the leaves.)

The first group to collect six leaves of the same color wins the game.

I will collect the leaves from the winning group and put them into the big bag. We will then continue the game, with the winning group choosing new leaves for its small bag.

▸ Begin the game and play for as long as time allows. Continue the game until the allotted time has elapsed.

CONCLUSION:

▸ Ask the students the following questions:

How did you feel when your group shared your leaves with another group?
(If the students felt a loss, explain that feeling a loss is an acceptable emotion because sharing involves making some kind of sacrifice or giving up something they enjoy.)

What helped your group collect several leaves of the same color?

LEAVES

YEAR-ROUND CLASSROOM GUIDANCE GAMES © 2007 MAR*CO PRODUCTS, INC. 1-800-448-2197

October

For Sail
Study Skills & Goal Setting
Columbus Day

Wild Thing's Choice
Responsible Decisions
Fall Celebration

In And Out Of The Corn Maze
Friendship
Fall

The Black Cat's Meow
Conflict Resolution
Halloween

FOR SAIL
Study Skills & Goal Setting/Columbus Day/Grades 3-5

PURPOSE:

To help students discover potential goals and learn what they must do to reach their goals

OBJECTIVE:

To set a life goal requiring at least two steps to reach

MATERIALS NEEDED:

For each student:
- ☐ 2 pieces of 8.5" x 11" construction paper
- ☐ Scissors
- ☐ Pencil
- ☐ Glue
- ☐ Crayons or markers

For the leader:
- ☐ 2 pieces of 8.5" x 11" construction paper
- ☐ Scissors
- ☐ Pencil
- ☐ Glue
- ☐ Crayons or markers

GAME PREPARATION:

Gather the necessary materials.

PROCEDURE:

▸ Ask the students to tell the group some things they know about Christopher Columbus. (He sailed to a new world, discovered new places, was determined, had problems, etc.)

▸ Continue by asking the following questions:

What things did Columbus have to do before he could set sail and discover new lands? (He needed to be seen as trustworthy; have a good reputation; have an education and skills; get money, supplies, and a crew; map his route; etc.)

What are some goals that you might like to reach in your life? A life goal could be a job you want to have when you grow up, a place you want to go, such as to college for further education, or how you want to live as an adult. Raise your hand if you have an idea you want to share with the group. (Acknowledge and discuss the responses. Let as many students as possible share their ideas. Encourage those who did not participate to think of goals for the future.)

▸ Distribute two pieces of construction paper, crayons or markers, scissors, and glue to each student. Make sure each student has a pencil.

▸ Say:

We are going to make sailboats out of construction paper. I will make one while you make yours. Follow these directions:

Fold the construction paper lengthwise, like a hot dog fold.

Fold the long open edges of the paper down to the fold.

Fold the four ends of the paper into triangles going down toward the first fold.

On another sheet of paper, draw a triangle. Cut it out and glue it to the open inside of the boat.

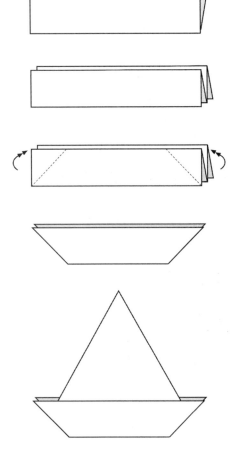

- Have each student use a pencil to write his/her goal on the pointed sail. When you are sure the spelling is correct, the students may use a marker or dark crayon to trace over the letters.

- On the sides of the sailboat, have each student write at least two things he/she will have to do to reach the goal on his/her sail. Tell the students to write one step on each side of the sailboat, using pencil first, then tracing over the letters with a marker or crayon. Then say:

   If your goal is to be a coach, you will need an education, knowledge of sports, and a good reputation. When you think of what you will need to do to reach your goal, think of the education and work skills you will need.

CONCLUSION:

- Have the students share their completed boats with the class.

WILD THING'S CHOICE
Responsible Decisions/Fall Celebration/Grades 3-5

PURPOSE:

To help students distinguish good decisions from poor decisions

OBJECTIVE:

For the class to reach predetermined points by having the students vote for the most appropriate decision

MATERIALS NEEDED:

For each student:
   None

For the leader:
   ☐ Wild Thing Mood Cards (page 31)
   ☐ Wild Thing Stick-Puppet Pattern (pages 32-33)
   ☐ Cardstock or paper
   ☐ Large craft or paint stick
   ☐ Scissors
   ☐ Markers
   ☐ Cardstock or paper and cardboard
   ☐ Glue
   ☐ Yarn, glitter, fabric (optional)
   ☐ Chalkboard and chalk

GAME PREPARATION:

Following the directions on page 32, make two Wild Thing Stick Puppets. Reproduce the Wild Thing Mood Cards on paper or cardstock and cut the cards apart. Laminate the cards for durability (optional).

PROCEDURE:

▸ Discuss appropriate and inappropriate decisions and the type of consequences that might result from inappropriate decisions. As an example, ask the students to suggest an appropriate and inappropriate decision about doing a homework assignment. Follow the students' suggestions with a discussion about the consequences each decision is likely to have.

▸ Tell the class:

> ***I will be reading a list of situations in which decisions must be made. Two students will be chosen to hold the Wild Thing Puppets and to make the decisions. Each puppet will react to the situation described by behaving according to the personality of the Wild Thing Mood Card drawn by the student holding that puppet. Each puppet volunteer will give his or her own unrehearsed reaction corresponding to the card drawn. For example, if the situation is about the class going on a field trip, the Wild Thing Puppet whose volunteer draws the Mean Mood Card might say, "That's dumb, it won't be any fun." The Wild Thing Puppet whose volunteer draws the Nice Mood card might say, "OK, I can learn a lot."*** (*Note:* If the puppet volunteer cannot think of a response, the class may volunteer suggestions.) ***After each Wild Thing Puppet has reacted to the situation, I will ask the students to vote, by putting thumbs up or thumbs down, for the response they feel is most appropriate. The majority vote will win.***

▸ Help the students decide how many points they think they could to earn in the allotted time. This number will be the point goal for the class. Record the point goal on the board.

▸ Randomly select two students to hold the Wild Thing Puppets. Place the mood cards face-down and have each student choose one card. Then select another student to stand midway between the two students holding the Wild Thing Puppets. This person lets one of the puppets peek over each of his/her shoulders. You may choose new volunteers after completing each situation.

▸ When the class chooses the Wild Thing Puppet that gave the appropriate response, award one point and record it on the board.

▸ Using the following situations, begin the game:

> Standing in the lunch line
> Sitting at the lunch table
> Cleaning up the lunch table
> Returning the lunch tray
> Coming into the classroom late
> Sharpening a pencil
> Walking to your desk
> Volunteering an answer
> Playing on the playground
> Doing classwork
> Walking down the hall

Playing with others
Going to the restroom
Coming into class in the morning
Being in the media center
Talking with friends in the lunchroom
Using the computer
Sitting in the school bus
Drawing
Singing
Listening to the teacher
Putting book bags on the shelf
Having a class party
Having a snack
Going on a field trip

▸ If the class reaches, exceeds, or comes close to the predetermined point goal let the students give themselves a cheer on the count of three.

CONCLUSION:

▸ Ask the students:

What helped you decide which puppet had a better response to the situations?

Who can tell us about a situation in which someone's inappropriate response made you feel uncomfortable?

NICE MOOD CARD

MEAN MOOD CARD

WILD THING STICK-PUPPET PATTERN

This simple two-sided stick puppet is easy to make.

Make two puppets.

1. Reproduce the puppet patterns on paper or cardstock.
2. If you reproduced the pattern on paper, glue the pattern to cardboard.
3. Color the Wild Things. You may also decorate the shape with yarn, glitter, fabric, etc., to enhance the design of the puppet.
4. Cut out the shape.
5. Glue one pattern to the front of a craft/paint stick. Glue the other pattern to the back.

IN AND OUT OF THE CORN MAZE
Friendship/Fall/Grades K-3

PURPOSE:

To help students recognize ways to *include* rather than *exclude* others

OBJECTIVE:

To gain the most team members

MATERIALS NEEDED:

For each student:
    None

For the leader:
    None

GAME PREPARATION:

None

PROCEDURE:

▸ Divide the class into two teams. (*Note*: It does not matter if the teams do not have the same number of members.)

▸ Have the members of one team form a circle by holding hands and raising their arms high into the air. This team will be the Corn Maze.

▸ Have the members of the other team form a straight line, holding onto each others' hands. This team will be the Travelers.

▸ Give the following directions:

> ***Beginning at any point outside the Corn Maze, the Travelers will move toward the center of the circle by ducking between and under the raised arms of two students. The Travelers will then go back out of the circle, moving between and under the raised arms of the next two members of***

the Corn Maze. The Travelers will work their way around the circle in this fashion. No member of either group may drop his or her arms or let go of his or her partners' hands.

As the Travelers move along the Corn Maze, I will read statements that either include or exclude others. The Corn Maze team must keep its arms up high so the Travelers can weave in and out of the circle whenever I read an including statement such as, "Ask a new person to play with you."

But, if I read an excluding statement such as, "I'm not going to play with you any more," the members of the Corn Maze team must lower their arms. Any Traveler caught in the middle of the circle when the members of the Corn Maze team lower their arms must join the Corn Maze team. When that happens, the two teams change positions.

The team with the most members at the end of playing time wins the game.

▸ Begin the game by calling out several *including statements.* Then call out an *excluding statement.* (*Note:* During the game you may repeat the statements.) Continue the game for as long as time allows. When the allotted time has elapsed, declare a winner.

INCLUDING	EXCLUDING
Do you need a pencil?	Leave me alone.
Let me help you.	You're nuts.
Will you be my friend?	I won't be your friend.
Do you want to play with us?	You're strange.
What is your name?	You can't play with us.
I like your book bag	That's a dumb shirt you're wearing.
Can you come to my house to play?	Stay away from her/him.
Can you come to my party?	I don't like you.
Would you help me?	You're ugly.
May I show you around?	Get out of here.
You go first, and I'll wait.	I'm first. I'm first.
Your haircut is great.	We don't have room for anyone else.

CONCLUSION:

▸ Ask the students the following questions:

How does it feel to be left out?

What are some things that you do or say to include others?

THE BLACK CAT'S MEOW
Conflict Resolution/Halloween/Grades 2-4

PURPOSE:

To help students learn positive ways to deal with conflict

OBJECTIVE:

To choose the cat that has the best response to a bad situation

MATERIALS NEEDED:

For each student:
    None

For the leader:
    ☐ Cat Masks (pages 39-41)
    ☐ Gray paper or cardstock
    ☐ Scissors
    ☐ 3 paint sticks
    ☐ Stapler and staples or glue

GAME PREPARATION:

Reproduce each Cat Mask on gray paper or gray cardstock. One cat is crying, another is angry and showing its teeth, and the third is wearing sunglasses to appear cool. Cut out the masks and holes for the eyes and mouth. Laminate the masks for durability. Staple or glue each mask to a paint stick.

PROCEDURE:

▸ Show the students the three cat masks. Tell the students:

I will choose three students to hold these masks. Then I will call out a situation and the three cats will respond. The mask that shows the crying black cat is named Weeping Cat. Each time I read a description of a situation, Weeping Cat will whine, "Meeooooow," as if his feelings have

been hurt. The mask that shows the angry cat is named Wild Cat. Each time I read a description of a situation, Wild Cat will make a hissing sound to show that he or she is angry. The mask that shows the cat with sunglasses is called Cool Cat. Each time I read a description of a situation, Cool Cat will call out, "Cool, Man," as if he or she is ignoring what I have said.

You will be divided into small groups of 3-5 students. You are to listen first to the situation, then to the responses of the cats. I will call on one group to respond to each situation by lining up behind the person whose mask is responding to the situation in what group members think is the best way. If the situation states, "Someone just shoved you out of line at the drinking fountain," the small group might line up behind the Wild Cat who responded with a hissing sound to show that it's wrong to shove people out of the way, behind the Weeping Cat to show that the cat's feelings were hurt, or behind the Cool Cat to show that the situation should be ignored. The group must decide if the situation would cause hurt feelings, make someone angry, or should just be ignored.

Then I will give each of the other small groups a chance to vote for or against the small group's choice. If your group agrees with the small group's decision, you will all make a pleasant meow sound when I call on you. If you disagree with the small group's choice, you will all make an angry hissing sound.

I will ask the members of the group standing to explain the reason for their choice. I will then ask the other groups why they agreed or disagreed with that group's choice. I may also ask what would happen if you chose one of the other cats. Any group whose members have a good reason for agreeing or disagreeing with the other group's choice will earn one point. It is possible for each group to earn a point each round.

The group with the most points at the end of the game is the winner.

▶ Divide the class into small groups of 3-5 members. Identify each group with a type of cat: Calico, Siamese, Angora, Tiger, Bobcat, Persian, Manx.

▶ Choose three people at random to hold the three cat masks. (*Note: You* may choose new players after completing each situation.)

▶ Begin the game by reading the following descriptions:

Someone makes fun of the way your mom looks.
A classmate grabs a crayon from your hand.
A friend laughs at you when you fall down in the hall.

The teacher yells at the whole class.
Someone makes fun of the lunch you brought from home.
A bigger classmate knocks you down on the playground.
A classmate rolls his/her eyes at you.
The teacher doesn't choose you to be the leader.
The teacher calls on someone else instead of you.
You don't feel like doing your classwork.
No one wants to play with you on the playground.
Your friend tells you he/she doesn't want to be your friend any more.
Someone says your art picture is ugly.
Someone crowds in front of you in line.

End the game after all of the situations have been read.

CONCLUSION:

▸ Ask the students:

Which situation was the hardest one for you to vote on?

Which situation was the easiest one for you to vote on?

Describe how you would feel in one of these situations.

WEEPING CAT MASK

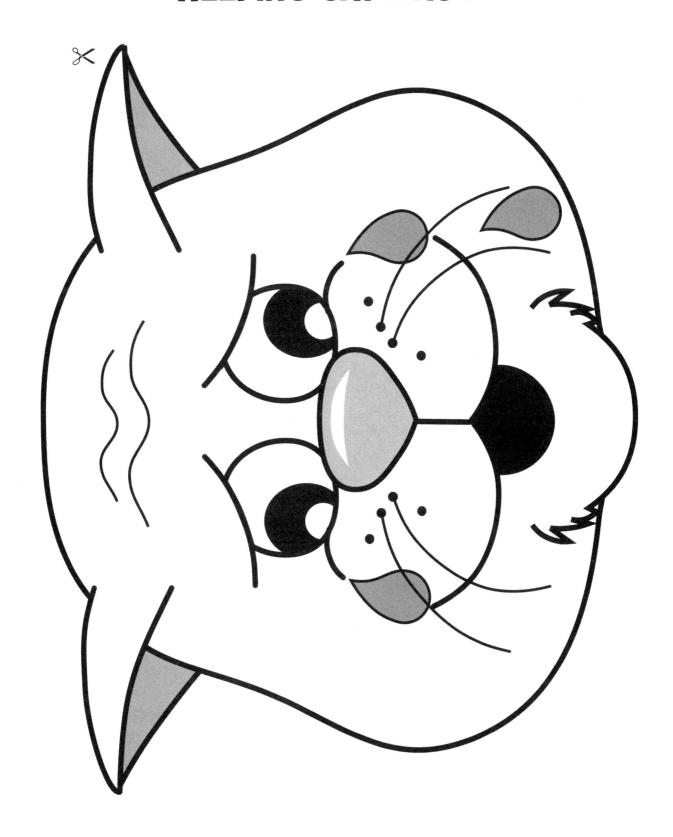

WILD CAT MASK

COOL CAT MASK

Vote For "Me-Ow"
Conflict Resolution
Election Day

Attention
Good Character
Veterans Day

Turkey Gobblie-Gook
Responsible Decisions
Thanksgiving

VOTE FOR "ME-OW"
Conflict Resolution/Election Day/Grades 3-5

PURPOSE:

To enable students to recognize acceptable and unacceptable responses to situations involving conflict

OBJECTIVE:

To earn the most Cat Treat Cards for your group by lining up behind the cat that correctly demonstrates the required category.

MATERIALS NEEDED:

For each student:
    None

For the leader:
    ☐ Cat Masks (pages 39-41)
    ☐ Cat Situation Cards (pages 48-49)
    ☐ Cat Treat Cards (page 50)
    ☐ Cardstock or paper
    ☐ 3 paint sticks
    ☐ Stapler and staples or glue
    ☐ Scissors
    ☐ Gray or tan paper or cardstock
    ☐ Chalkboard and chalk

GAME PREPARATION:

Reproduce each Cat Mask on gray or tan paper or cardstock. One cat is crying. Another is angry and showing its teeth, and the third is wearing sunglasses to appear cool. Cut out the masks and holes for the eyes and mouth. Laminate the masks for durability. Staple or glue each mask to a paint stick. Reproduce the Cat Situation Cards and the Cat Treat Cards on paper or cardstock and cut them apart. Laminate the cards for durability (optional).

PROCEDURE:

▸ Begin the lesson by asking the students:

What is the definition of the word conflict? (Disagreement, fight, showing dislike for someone, etc.)

▸ Have the students give examples of acceptable ways to react to a conflict situation and examples of unacceptable ways to react to a conflict situation.

▸ Then say:

Since this is the time of year that adults exercise free choice and vote to elect government officials or leaders, we are going to practice our free choice by voting.

▸ Divide the class into small groups of 3-5 members. Give each group a number to differentiate it from another group. (*Note:* For fun, you might want to give each group the name of a different breed of cat, such as Calico, Siamese, Angora, Tiger, Bobcat, Persian, Manx.)

▸ Showing the students the three masks, say:

I will choose three students to stand in the front of the room and hold these masks. The mask that shows the crying cat is named Weeping Cat Each time I read a description of a situation, Weeping Cat will whine "Meeooow" and respond to the situation in a way that shows he or she is not trying to help him or herself. The mask that shows the growling cat showing its teeth is named Wild Cat. Each time I read a description of a situation, Wild Cat will make a hissing sound and respond to the situation in a way that shows he or she is looking for a fight or trying to scare someone away. The mask that shows the cat wearing sunglasses is called Cool Cat. Each time I read a description of a situation, Cool Cat will say "Cool, Man" and respond to the situation in a calm, relaxed way.

▸ Ask each student holding a mask to show how he/she is going to react to the situations when read.

▸ Continue explaining the activity by saying:

I will be reading aloud from a Cat Situation Card and a Cat Treat Card. The words on the Cat Situation Card will describe something someone is saying. The Cat Treat Card will request a certain category. Calling on each group by number (or cat name), I will instruct group members to line up behind the cat mask that represents the required category. This will be like voting for your favorite candidate. Each group lined up behind the cat

with the correct response will earn one point. There may be more than one answer for some of the Cat Treat Cards. Here is how that could work:

Suppose the Cat Situation Card read, "Get out of my way or I'll push you out of line" and the Cat Treat Card read, "The silliest answer." Your group would need to line up behind the cat mask that has the silliest response to that specific situation. I will decide if your choice makes sense. I may ask you why you felt this was the best choice.

At the end of our time, each group will add up the number of points it has earned. The group with the most points will be the winning group. Remember: the Wild Cat is not always a poor response. It can be the best response if you need to be assertive to show someone that he or she is wrong.

▸ Write each team's name or number on the board. Then begin the game by drawing one Cat Situation Card and a Cat Treat Card. Read the Cat Situation Card, then put it aside. Each Cat Situation Card should only be read once. Read the Cat Treat Card and put it on the bottom of the pile. You may shuffle the Cat Treat Cards or just put them on the bottom of the pile and use each card twice. Record each team's points on the board as they earn them. Continue the game until all of the Cat Situation Cards have been read or the allotted time has elapsed.

CONCLUSION:

▸ Ask the students:

Which situation would be the most hurtful for you?

What is the best response for you to make in a conflict?

How did it feel to vote for your choice?

What would you do if someone said to you, "You are such a tattle tale."

CAT SITUATION CARD/YEAR-ROUND CLASSROOM GUIDANCE GAMES
© 2007 MAR•CO PRODUCTS, INC. 1-800-448-2197

What would you do if someone said to you, "Let me copy your answers."

CAT SITUATION CARD/YEAR-ROUND CLASSROOM GUIDANCE GAMES
© 2007 MAR•CO PRODUCTS, INC. 1-800-448-2197

What would you do if someone said to you, "Nobody likes you."

CAT SITUATION CARD/YEAR-ROUND CLASSROOM GUIDANCE GAMES
© 2007 MAR•CO PRODUCTS, INC. 1-800-448-2197

What would you do if someone said to you, "I'm not going to play with you any more."

CAT SITUATION CARD/YEAR-ROUND CLASSROOM GUIDANCE GAMES
© 2007 MAR•CO PRODUCTS, INC. 1-800-448-2197

What would you do if someone said to you, "I'm having a birthday party, but you're not invited."

CAT SITUATION CARD/YEAR-ROUND CLASSROOM GUIDANCE GAMES
© 2007 MAR•CO PRODUCTS, INC. 1-800-448-2197

What would you do if someone said to you, "Keep away from me."

CAT SITUATION CARD/YEAR-ROUND CLASSROOM GUIDANCE GAMES
© 2007 MAR•CO PRODUCTS, INC. 1-800-448-2197

What would you do if someone said to you, "Why are your ears so big?"

CAT SITUATION CARD/YEAR-ROUND CLASSROOM GUIDANCE GAMES
© 2007 MAR•CO PRODUCTS, INC. 1-800-448-2197

What would you do if someone said to you, "Why don't you stop hanging around me. I really don't like you."

CAT SITUATION CARD/YEAR-ROUND CLASSROOM GUIDANCE GAMES
© 2007 MAR•CO PRODUCTS, INC. 1-800-448-2197

What would you do if you got a bad grade on a math test and someone said to you, "I guess you're not very smart in math."

CAT SITUATION CARD/YEAR-ROUND CLASSROOM GUIDANCE GAMES
© 2007 MAR•CO PRODUCTS, INC. 1-800-448-2197

What would you do if someone said to you, "I know you said it was a secret, but I decided to tell anyway."

CAT SITUATION CARD/YEAR-ROUND CLASSROOM GUIDANCE GAMES
© 2007 MAR•CO PRODUCTS, INC. 1-800-448-2197

What would you do if someone said to you, "I'm tired of always playing your favorite game."

CAT SITUATION CARD/YEAR-ROUND CLASSROOM GUIDANCE GAMES
© 2007 MAR•CO PRODUCTS, INC. 1-800-448-2197

What would you do if someone said to you, "Stop bugging me."

CAT SITUATION CARD/YEAR-ROUND CLASSROOM GUIDANCE GAMES
© 2007 MAR•CO PRODUCTS, INC. 1-800-448-2197

What would you do if someone said to you, "I knew the answers, and you didn't know any."

CAT SITUATION CARD/YEAR-ROUND CLASSROOM GUIDANCE GAMES
© 2007 MAR•CO PRODUCTS, INC. 1-800-448-2197

What would you do if someone said to you, "That picture you made in art looks silly."

CAT SITUATION CARD/YEAR-ROUND CLASSROOM GUIDANCE GAMES
© 2007 MAR•CO PRODUCTS, INC. 1-800-448-2197

What would you do if someone said to you, "That shirt you have on looks old and junky."

CAT SITUATION CARD/YEAR-ROUND CLASSROOM GUIDANCE GAMES
© 2007 MAR•CO PRODUCTS, INC. 1-800-448-2197

What would you do if someone said to you, "Guess what? I heard the teacher say she doesn't like you."

CAT SITUATION CARD/YEAR-ROUND CLASSROOM GUIDANCE GAMES
© 2007 MAR•CO PRODUCTS, INC. 1-800-448-2197

What would you do if someone said to you, "You're always in trouble. That's why you get your name on the board all the time."

CAT SITUATION CARD/YEAR-ROUND CLASSROOM GUIDANCE GAMES
© 2007 MAR•CO PRODUCTS, INC. 1-800-448-2197

What would you do if someone said to you, "I can't imagine why you didn't get invited to the party."

CAT SITUATION CARD/YEAR-ROUND CLASSROOM GUIDANCE GAMES
© 2007 MAR•CO PRODUCTS, INC. 1-800-448-2197

What would you do if someone said to you, "You are always complaining about something. That's why you don't have any friends."

CAT SITUATION CARD/YEAR-ROUND CLASSROOM GUIDANCE GAMES
© 2007 MAR•CO PRODUCTS, INC. 1-800-448-2197

What would you say if someone said to you, "You're a bully."

CAT SITUATION CARD/YEAR-ROUND CLASSROOM GUIDANCE GAMES
© 2007 MAR•CO PRODUCTS, INC. 1-800-448-2197

Silliest
Response

Ugliest
Response

Happiest
Response

Best
Response

Most Correct
Response

Incorrect
Response

Poorest-Mannered
Response

Most Hateful
Response

Laughable
Response

Unnecessary
Response

ATTENTION
Good Character/Veterans Day/Grades 3-5

PURPOSE:

To help students identify the qualities that make our country strong

OBJECTIVE:

To give the students an opportunity to demonstrate
good character traits and explain the importance of each

MATERIALS NEEDED:

For each student:
    None

For the leader:
    ☐ Good Character Cards (page 53)
    ☐ Cardstock or paper
    ☐ Timer
    ☐ Scissors

GAME PREPARATION:

Reproduce two copies of the Good Character Cards on paper or cardstock and cut the cards apart. Laminate the cards for durability (optional).

PROCEDURE:

▸ Have the students raise their hands if someone in their family is or has been in some branch of the military. (Acknowledge the show of hands.)

▸ Have each student tell which branch of the Armed Services his/her family member represents. (Mention the Air Force, Marines, Army, Navy, Coast Guard, and Special Services.)

▶ Ask:

What are some good character qualities that you believe members of these branches of service display? (Good hygiene, good listening skills, obedience, following directions and orders, patriotism, etc.)

▶ Explain the game procedure:

I will pair you with another person who is sitting near you. Each pair will receive a Good Character Card with a character trait. Another pair of students will also receive the same Good Character Card. Each pair will have three minutes to read the Good Character Card and decide how they would demonstrate that character trait. Talk with your partner about why the character trait you have been assigned is important for someone who is in the military.

After you and your partner have worked together for three minutes, I will pair you both with other partners who have the same character trait. This new group of four will then have three minutes to decide how they would demonstrate the assigned character trait and tell why they think that trait is important for someone in military service to have.

After three minutes, I will pair each group of four with another group of partners, forming a group of eight. Then the four students within this group assigned the same character trait will have four minutes to demonstrate their character trait to the other four students, having them guess which character trait they are portraying, then explaining why it is a good trait for someone in military service to have. Then the other four students will repeat the process, demonstrating their assigned character trait.

Then we will share, as a class, what each group learned about what good character is and how it relates to military service.

▶ Divide the students into pairs. Distribute a Good Character Card to each pair, making sure that two pairs receive the same Good Character Card. Be sure to know which pair has which character trait so you can easily move the pairs into groups of four. Tell the students to begin the game. Begin timing and continue to do so until the class has come together as a large group.

CONCLUSION:

▶ Ask the students the following question:

Which good character traits important to men and women in the military are also important for us in our daily lives? Why?

Hard-Working

Brave

Cooperative

Kind

Responsible

Respectful

Disciplined

Obedient

Patriotic

Dependable

TURKEY GOBBLIE-GOOK
Responsible Decisions/Thanksgiving/Grades 2-5

PURPOSE:

To teach students to recognize poor decisions

OBJECTIVE:

To win by finding the most turkeys

MATERIALS NEEDED:

For each student:
  None

For the leader:
  ☐ Gobblie-Gook Poor Decision Cards (pages 56-57)
  ☐ Turkey Cards (page 58)
  ☐ Cardstock or paper
  ☐ Scissors

GAME PREPARATION:

Reproduce 12 sets of the Turkey Cards (120 cards) on paper or cardstock. Reproduce the Gobblie-Gook Poor Decision Cards on paper or cardstock. (*Note:* You may use the blank card to write an additional situation.) Cut the cards apart. Laminate the cards for durability (optional).

PROCEDURE:

▸ Distribute three Turkey Cards to each player. Explain that some are marked with a star for protection. Tell the students not to show their Turkey Cards to anyone. Put the rest of the Turkey Cards in a pile on the leader's desk.

▸ Explain the game by saying:

   I will read a Gobblie-Gook Poor Decision Card aloud to the first player seated in a row. That person gets a chance to give a reasonable explanation of why the decision was a poor decision.

If I determine the player has given a reasonable answer, he or she may choose one Turkey Card from any other player. The chosen player must give up the card unless it has a protective star on it. Then the player who gave up a card chooses another Turkey Card from the stack. If the card has a protective star, the player who answered the Gobblie-Gook Poor Decision Card may ask one other player for a card. If that player also has a card with a protective star, the game will go on, and the player will not receive an additional card for that round.

Then I will repeat the process with the student seated behind the previous player. When I reach the end of one row, I will continue with the first person in the next row. We will continue to play the game until every student has had a chance to play the game. The person with the most Turkey Cards at the end of the activity wins.

▸ Begin the game. After each student has had a chance to respond to a card, declare the student with the most Turkey Cards the winner.

CONCLUSION:

▸ Ask the students:

How did good listening help you play this game?

Why do you need good listening skills to recognize poor decisions?

No one will speak
to a new classmate
because he/she
doesn't look like
the other students.

GOBBLIE-GOOK POOR DECISION CARD
YEAR-ROUND CLASSROOM GUIDANCE GAMES
© 2007 MAR•CO PRODUCTS, INC. 1-800-448-2197

Someone
deliberately kicks
someone else on
the school bus.

GOBBLIE-GOOK POOR DECISION CARD
YEAR-ROUND CLASSROOM GUIDANCE GAMES
© 2007 MAR•CO PRODUCTS, INC. 1-800-448-2197

Someone yells
angrily at
another person.

GOBBLIE-GOOK POOR DECISION CARD
YEAR-ROUND CLASSROOM GUIDANCE GAMES
© 2007 MAR•CO PRODUCTS, INC. 1-800-448-2197

Someone tells
lies about
a classmate.

GOBBLIE-GOOK POOR DECISION CARD
YEAR-ROUND CLASSROOM GUIDANCE GAMES
© 2007 MAR•CO PRODUCTS, INC. 1-800-448-2197

Someone runs
down the halls.

GOBBLIE-GOOK POOR DECISION CARD
YEAR-ROUND CLASSROOM GUIDANCE GAMES
© 2007 MAR•CO PRODUCTS, INC. 1-800-448-2197

Someone
runs into the
Media Center.

GOBBLIE-GOOK POOR DECISION CARD
YEAR-ROUND CLASSROOM GUIDANCE GAMES
© 2007 MAR•CO PRODUCTS, INC. 1-800-448-2197

Someone
throws food
in the cafeteria.

GOBBLIE-GOOK POOR DECISION CARD
YEAR-ROUND CLASSROOM GUIDANCE GAMES
© 2007 MAR•CO PRODUCTS, INC. 1-800-448-2197

Someone
pushes
everyone
in line.

GOBBLIE-GOOK POOR DECISION CARD
YEAR-ROUND CLASSROOM GUIDANCE GAMES
© 2007 MAR•CO PRODUCTS, INC. 1-800-448-2197

Someone spreads
an unkind rumor
about a classmate.

GOBBLIE-GOOK POOR DECISION CARD
YEAR-ROUND CLASSROOM GUIDANCE GAMES
© 2007 MAR•CO PRODUCTS, INC. 1-800-448-2197

Someone
cheats
on a test.

GOBBLIE-GOOK POOR DECISION CARD
YEAR-ROUND CLASSROOM GUIDANCE GAMES
© 2007 MAR•CO PRODUCTS, INC. 1-800-448-2197

A student hasn't completed his/her homework.

GOBBLIE-GOOK POOR DECISION CARD
YEAR-ROUND CLASSROOM GUIDANCE GAMES
© 2007 MAR*CO PRODUCTS, INC. 1-800-448-2197

A student doesn't finish his/her classwork.

GOBBLIE-GOOK POOR DECISION CARD
YEAR-ROUND CLASSROOM GUIDANCE GAMES
© 2007 MAR*CO PRODUCTS, INC. 1-800-448-2197

Students do not listen to the teacher.

GOBBLIE-GOOK POOR DECISION CARD
YEAR-ROUND CLASSROOM GUIDANCE GAMES
© 2007 MAR*CO PRODUCTS, INC. 1-800-448-2197

Everyone is too loud in the cafeteria.

GOBBLIE-GOOK POOR DECISION CARD
YEAR-ROUND CLASSROOM GUIDANCE GAMES
© 2007 MAR*CO PRODUCTS, INC. 1-800-448-2197

Some students leave a mess in the restroom.

GOBBLIE-GOOK POOR DECISION CARD
YEAR-ROUND CLASSROOM GUIDANCE GAMES
© 2007 MAR*CO PRODUCTS, INC. 1-800-448-2197

Everyone in the class makes too much noise in the hall.

GOBBLIE-GOOK POOR DECISION CARD
YEAR-ROUND CLASSROOM GUIDANCE GAMES
© 2007 MAR*CO PRODUCTS, INC. 1-800-448-2197

Two students fight on the playground.

GOBBLIE-GOOK POOR DECISION CARD
YEAR-ROUND CLASSROOM GUIDANCE GAMES
© 2007 MAR*CO PRODUCTS, INC. 1-800-448-2197

Two students watch another student bully a younger child.

GOBBLIE-GOOK POOR DECISION CARD
YEAR-ROUND CLASSROOM GUIDANCE GAMES
© 2007 MAR*CO PRODUCTS, INC. 1-800-448-2197

A student copies another student's homework.

GOBBLIE-GOOK POOR DECISION CARD
YEAR-ROUND CLASSROOM GUIDANCE GAMES
© 2007 MAR*CO PRODUCTS, INC. 1-800-448-2197

GOBBLIE-GOOK POOR DECISION CARD
YEAR-ROUND CLASSROOM GUIDANCE GAMES
© 2007 MAR*CO PRODUCTS, INC. 1-800-448-2197

TURKEY CARD/YEAR-ROUND CLASSROOM GUIDANCE GAMES
© 2007 MAR*CO PRODUCTS, INC. 1-800-448-2197

TURKEY CARD/YEAR-ROUND CLASSROOM GUIDANCE GAMES
© 2007 MAR*CO PRODUCTS, INC. 1-800-448-2197

TURKEY CARD/YEAR-ROUND CLASSROOM GUIDANCE GAMES
© 2007 MAR*CO PRODUCTS, INC. 1-800-448-2197

TURKEY CARD/YEAR-ROUND CLASSROOM GUIDANCE GAMES
© 2007 MAR*CO PRODUCTS, INC. 1-800-448-2197

TURKEY CARD/YEAR-ROUND CLASSROOM GUIDANCE GAMES
© 2007 MAR*CO PRODUCTS, INC. 1-800-448-2197

TURKEY CARD/YEAR-ROUND CLASSROOM GUIDANCE GAMES
© 2007 MAR*CO PRODUCTS, INC. 1-800-448-2197

TURKEY CARD/YEAR-ROUND CLASSROOM GUIDANCE GAMES
© 2007 MAR*CO PRODUCTS, INC. 1-800-448-2197

TURKEY CARD/YEAR-ROUND CLASSROOM GUIDANCE GAMES
© 2007 MAR*CO PRODUCTS, INC. 1-800-448-2197

TURKEY CARD/YEAR-ROUND CLASSROOM GUIDANCE GAMES
© 2007 MAR*CO PRODUCTS, INC. 1-800-448-2197

TURKEY CARD/YEAR-ROUND CLASSROOM GUIDANCE GAMES
© 2007 MAR*CO PRODUCTS, INC. 1-800-448-2197

December

Here Comes Frosty
Social Skills
Holiday Season

Sharing Candy Canes
Social Skills
Holiday Season

HERE COMES FROSTY
Social Skills/Holiday Season/Grades K-2

PURPOSE:

To teach students to explain what has been done wrong or right by reacting with good or bad manners

OBJECTIVE:

To be able to continue to be a snowman/woman for three rounds

MATERIALS NEEDED:

For each student:
  None

For the leader:
  ☐ Good/Bad Manners Cards (pages 64-65)
  ☐ Cardstock or paper
  ☐ Scissors

GAME PREPARATION:

Reproduce the Good/Bad Manners Cards on paper or cardstock and cut the cards apart. Laminate the cards for durability (optional).

PROCEDURE:

▸ Introduce the game by saying:

> **At this time of year, many children hope to receive gifts. Do you know what someone might do in order to not receive the gifts they want?** (Children who are naughty may not receive the gifts they want.)

▸ Explain activity by saying:

Our lesson today is about manners. I have a list of situations in which everyone uses manners. Sometimes they use good manners and sometimes they use bad manners. Our activity today will help us learn the difference between good and bad manners. The snowmen and snowwomen and their snowflake helpers will help us learn this lesson.

I will choose three of you to come to the front of the room to be a snowman or snowwoman named Frosty.

Each Frosty will have snowflakes to help him or her, and I will choose three of you to be snowflakes. The three snowflakes will draw one card from the stack of Manners Cards. Only the snowflakes will know whether the card they choose says Good Manners or Bad Manners, and the snowflakes must keep the card a secret from the Frosties and the rest of the class. If the snowflakes draw a card that says Good Manners, they will talk quietly among themselves and decide what would show good manners in the situation I read. If the three snowflakes draw a card that says Bad Manners, they will talk quietly among themselves and decide what would show bad manners in the situation. The three snowflakes will decide what to say. The snowflakes' spokesperson will tell the Frosties what they would do in the situation I read, based on the card they drew.

When the snowflakes' spokesperson has finished describing what they would do, I will say, "Here comes Frosty." If the snowflakes use bad manners, all three Frosties must call out, "No gifts" at the same time. If the snowflakes use good manners, the Frosties will call out, "Gifts."

All three Frosty's must call out as soon as I say, "Here Comes Frosty." If they do not, they will lose their Frosty positions. All three Frosties must give the answer I determine to be the correct answer. If they do not all give the correct answer, all three Frosties will lose their positions. The Frosties may not discuss with each other what they are going to say. If they lose their positions, new Frosties will replace them and three new snowflakes will also be chosen to come to the front of the room. Remember, even one wrong response from the Frosty group sends all three Frosties back to their seats.

After one group of Frosties has given three correct answers, those Frosties retire and three new Frosties take their places. The goal is to try to be a group of Frosties that stays in place for three rounds of play. The snowflakes, stay or leave when the Frosties do.

▸ Begin the game by choosing the first three Frosties and the first three snowflakes. Pause after reading each Manners Situation.

▸ Manners Situations: (Each of these may be used more than once.)

Walking down the hall behind someone
Coming into the Media Center
Being served cafeteria food that you don't like
Having a classroom visitor
Having the teacher assign classwork
Singing a song you don't like
Not being called on to answer a question when your hand is raised
Sitting beside a classmate who treats you badly
Sitting on the bus next to someone you don't like
Eating your lunch
Being introduced to someone
Listening to announcements on the intercom
Watching announcements on the classroom TV

Continue the game for as long as time allows.

CONCLUSION:

▸ Ask the students:

How do you feel when you use good manners?

How do you feel when you use bad manners?

Who can describe a situation in which you saw someone using good manners or bad manners?

GOOD MANNERS CARD/YEAR-ROUND CLASSROOM GUIDANCE GAMES
© 2007 MAR*CO PRODUCTS, INC. 1-800-448-2197

GOOD MANNERS CARD/YEAR-ROUND CLASSROOM GUIDANCE GAMES
© 2007 MAR*CO PRODUCTS, INC. 1-800-448-2197

GOOD MANNERS CARD/YEAR-ROUND CLASSROOM GUIDANCE GAMES
© 2007 MAR*CO PRODUCTS, INC. 1-800-448-2197

GOOD MANNERS CARD/YEAR-ROUND CLASSROOM GUIDANCE GAMES
© 2007 MAR*CO PRODUCTS, INC. 1-800-448-2197

GOOD MANNERS CARD/YEAR-ROUND CLASSROOM GUIDANCE GAMES
© 2007 MAR*CO PRODUCTS, INC. 1-800-448-2197

GOOD MANNERS CARD/YEAR-ROUND CLASSROOM GUIDANCE GAMES
© 2007 MAR*CO PRODUCTS, INC. 1-800-448-2197

GOOD MANNERS CARD/YEAR-ROUND CLASSROOM GUIDANCE GAMES
© 2007 MAR*CO PRODUCTS, INC. 1-800-448-2197

GOOD MANNERS CARD/YEAR-ROUND CLASSROOM GUIDANCE GAMES
© 2007 MAR*CO PRODUCTS, INC. 1-800-448-2197

GOOD MANNERS CARD/YEAR-ROUND CLASSROOM GUIDANCE GAMES
© 2007 MAR*CO PRODUCTS, INC. 1-800-448-2197

GOOD MANNERS CARD/YEAR-ROUND CLASSROOM GUIDANCE GAMES
© 2007 MAR*CO PRODUCTS, INC. 1-800-448-2197

BAD MANNERS CARD/YEAR-ROUND CLASSROOM GUIDANCE GAMES
© 2007 MAR•CO PRODUCTS, INC. 1-800-448-2197

BAD MANNERS CARD/YEAR-ROUND CLASSROOM GUIDANCE GAMES
© 2007 MAR•CO PRODUCTS, INC. 1-800-448-2197

BAD MANNERS CARD/YEAR-ROUND CLASSROOM GUIDANCE GAMES
© 2007 MAR•CO PRODUCTS, INC. 1-800-448-2197

BAD MANNERS CARD/YEAR-ROUND CLASSROOM GUIDANCE GAMES
© 2007 MAR•CO PRODUCTS, INC. 1-800-448-2197

BAD MANNERS CARD/YEAR-ROUND CLASSROOM GUIDANCE GAMES
© 2007 MAR•CO PRODUCTS, INC. 1-800-448-2197

BAD MANNERS CARD/YEAR-ROUND CLASSROOM GUIDANCE GAMES
© 2007 MAR•CO PRODUCTS, INC. 1-800-448-2197

BAD MANNERS CARD/YEAR-ROUND CLASSROOM GUIDANCE GAMES
© 2007 MAR•CO PRODUCTS, INC. 1-800-448-2197

BAD MANNERS CARD/YEAR-ROUND CLASSROOM GUIDANCE GAMES
© 2007 MAR•CO PRODUCTS, INC. 1-800-448-2197

BAD MANNERS CARD/YEAR-ROUND CLASSROOM GUIDANCE GAMES
© 2007 MAR•CO PRODUCTS, INC. 1-800-448-2197

BAD MANNERS CARD/YEAR-ROUND CLASSROOM GUIDANCE GAMES
© 2007 MAR•CO PRODUCTS, INC. 1-800-448-2197

SHARING CANDY CANES
Social Skills/Holiday Season/Grades 3-5

PURPOSE:

To teach students to recognize ways they can share with others

OBJECTIVE:

To earn the most points for your small group by guessing what is being shared

MATERIALS NEEDED:

For each student:
    None

For the leader:
- ☐ Candy Cane Action Cards (page 68)
- ☐ Candy Cane Cards (page 69)
- ☐ Cardstock or paper
- ☐ Scissors
- ☐ Chalkboard and chalk

GAME PREPARATION:

Reproduce the Candy Cane Action Cards on paper or cardstock. Reproduce enough Candy Cane Cards on paper or cardstock for each group to have one Candy Cane Card for each Candy Cane Action Card used in the activity. For example, if you divide 30 students into groups of five, you will need six Candy Cane Cards for each Candy Cane Action Card used. Cut the cards apart. Laminate the cards for durability (optional).

PROCEDURE:

▸ Have the students describe different ways they share. (Share toys, money, things, time, talent, good attitude, kindness, friendship, helping others, etc.) Write their answers on the board.

▸ Divide the students into small groups of 3-5 members.

▸ Explain the activity by saying:

We are going to continue learning about sharing. I will give each group a chance to role-play one of the Candy Cane Action Cards. These cards describe an idea and a setting for showing one way to share. The words underlined in the little play described on the Candy Cane Action Card are the answers to your play. You must not say these words. You want the other class members to say these words.

When one group finishes presenting its play, the other groups should decide among themselves what is being shared in the play. After the groups have decided on an answer, one person from each group should come to the front of the room and whisper the group's answer to me. Every group that gives the correct answer receives a Candy Cane Card. The group that presented the play also receives a Candy Cane Card.

The team or teams with the most Candy Cane Cards will win the game.

▸ Begin the game. After each group has presented its play, declare the team or teams with the most Candy Cane Cards the winner(s).

CONCLUSION:

▸ Ask the students:

How important is it to share with others? Why?

What do you share best? Why?

Share a helping hand by opening a door for someone who has a lot to carry.

CANDY CANE ACTION CARD
YEAR-ROUND CLASSROOM GUIDANCE GAMES
© 2007 MAR•CO PRODUCTS, INC. 1-800-448-2197

Share a good, happy attitude with your parents when they ask you to clean your room.

CANDY CANE ACTION CARD
YEAR-ROUND CLASSROOM GUIDANCE GAMES
© 2007 MAR•CO PRODUCTS, INC. 1-800-448-2197

Share kind words with someone, such as complimenting your parents on the good meal.

CANDY CANE ACTION CARD
YEAR-ROUND CLASSROOM GUIDANCE GAMES
© 2007 MAR•CO PRODUCTS, INC. 1-800-448-2197

Share a greeting such as "Hi" or "Good morning" with a classmate in the hall.

CANDY CANE ACTION CARD
YEAR-ROUND CLASSROOM GUIDANCE GAMES
© 2007 MAR•CO PRODUCTS, INC. 1-800-448-2197

Share a song (or other talent) with your friends.

CANDY CANE ACTION CARD
YEAR-ROUND CLASSROOM GUIDANCE GAMES
© 2007 MAR•CO PRODUCTS, INC. 1-800-448-2197

Share money by making a donation to a charity.

CANDY CANE ACTION CARD
YEAR-ROUND CLASSROOM GUIDANCE GAMES
© 2007 MAR•CO PRODUCTS, INC. 1-800-448-2197

Share clothes by cleaning out your closet and giving things you've outgrown to a charity.

CANDY CANE ACTION CARD
YEAR-ROUND CLASSROOM GUIDANCE GAMES
© 2007 MAR•CO PRODUCTS, INC. 1-800-448-2197

Share a friendship by showing a new schoolmate where to find things.

CANDY CANE ACTION CARD
YEAR-ROUND CLASSROOM GUIDANCE GAMES
© 2007 MAR•CO PRODUCTS, INC. 1-800-448-2197

Share a favorite toy with visiting friends.

CANDY CANE ACTION CARD
YEAR-ROUND CLASSROOM GUIDANCE GAMES
© 2007 MAR•CO PRODUCTS, INC. 1-800-448-2197

Share your time by visiting an elderly person or someone who can't get out much.

CANDY CANE ACTION CARD
YEAR-ROUND CLASSROOM GUIDANCE GAMES
© 2007 MAR•CO PRODUCTS, INC. 1-800-448-2197

CANDY CANE CARD
YEAR-ROUND CLASSROOM GUIDANCE GAMES
© 2007 MAR∗CO PRODUCTS, INC. 1-800-448-2197

CANDY CANE CARD
YEAR-ROUND CLASSROOM GUIDANCE GAMES
© 2007 MAR∗CO PRODUCTS, INC. 1-800-448-2197

CANDY CANE CARD
YEAR-ROUND CLASSROOM GUIDANCE GAMES
© 2007 MAR∗CO PRODUCTS, INC. 1-800-448-2197

CANDY CANE CARD
YEAR-ROUND CLASSROOM GUIDANCE GAMES
© 2007 MAR∗CO PRODUCTS, INC. 1-800-448-2197

CANDY CANE CARD
YEAR-ROUND CLASSROOM GUIDANCE GAMES
© 2007 MAR∗CO PRODUCTS, INC. 1-800-448-2197

CANDY CANE CARD
YEAR-ROUND CLASSROOM GUIDANCE GAMES
© 2007 MAR∗CO PRODUCTS, INC. 1-800-448-2197

CANDY CANE CARD
YEAR-ROUND CLASSROOM GUIDANCE GAMES
© 2007 MAR∗CO PRODUCTS, INC. 1-800-448-2197

CANDY CANE CARD
YEAR-ROUND CLASSROOM GUIDANCE GAMES
© 2007 MAR∗CO PRODUCTS, INC. 1-800-448-2197

CANDY CANE CARD
YEAR-ROUND CLASSROOM GUIDANCE GAMES
© 2007 MAR∗CO PRODUCTS, INC. 1-800-448-2197

CANDY CANE CARD
YEAR-ROUND CLASSROOM GUIDANCE GAMES
© 2007 MAR∗CO PRODUCTS, INC. 1-800-448-2197

JANUARY

Shine On Me
Responsible Decisions
New Year

Red Light, Green Light
Conflict Resolution
Martin Luther King Jr. Day

Snowball A Friend
Friendship
Winter

SHINE ON ME
Responsible Decisions/New Year/Grades K-4

PURPOSE:

To teach students to recognize positive and negative decisions

OBJECTIVE:

To match the most negative and positive decisions by choosing two players with matching decision cards

MATERIALS NEEDED:

For each student:
    None

For the leader:
- ☐ Flashlight Cards (pages 75-77)
- ☐ Cardstock or paper
- ☐ Scissors
- ☐ Flashlight

GAME PREPARATION:

Reproduce two copies of the Flashlight Cards on paper or cardstock and cut the cards apart. Laminate the cards for durability (optional). Select one match for each participating student. Shuffle the cards. Gather the other materials.

PROCEDURE:

▸ Introduce the activity by saying:

This is a new year. Many people make New Year's resolutions. What do you think New Year's resolutions are? (Good things that people say they are going to do.)

Yes. These are positive decisions or resolutions for the New Year.

What are some New Year's resolutions that you have made or that you have heard others make?

▸ Explain the activity:

In today's game, each player will have a Flashlight Card that matches someone else's Flashlight Card. When you receive your card, do not show it to anyone else.

The person chosen to be "It" will have the flashlight. "It" will shine the flashlight on two different players. Those players will read aloud the number and the decision on their Flashlight Cards. (*Note:* Be ready to help the students read the cards if necessary. The numbers have been printed on the cards to help non-readers determine if there is a match.) *If the decisions on the two cards match, "It" must say whether it is a good, positive, or happy decision or a bad, negative, or unhappy decision. If I decide "It's" answer is correct, "It" gets the two cards and another turn to shine the flashlight on two other players. The players who gave their cards to "It" each choose another Flashlight Card from the deck.*

If there is no match, "It" chooses another player who has not already had a turn to be "It."

The winner will be the person with the most matching cards.

▸ Choose a student to be "It." Give a Flashlight Card to each player, including "It." Remind the group to listen and remember what cards the other players have, so any player who becomes "It" will be able to make a match more easily. Begin the game and play for as long as time allows. When the allotted time has elapsed, declare a winner. If time runs out before each student has had a chance to participate, declare a winner for the day. Then tell the students that they will play the game another day, and those students who did not get a chance to play, will get to go first next time.

CONCLUSION:

▸ Have the students:

Describe how negative or unhappy decisions make them feel and give an example of a time a decision made them feel this way.

Describe how positive, happy decisions, or good New Year's resolutions make them feel and give an example of a time a decision made them feel this way.

Crying every morning in class because you want to go home

1

FLASHLIGHT CARD
YEAR-ROUND CLASSROOM GUIDANCE GAMES
© 2007 MAR∗CO PRODUCTS, INC. 1-800-448-2197

Sleeping in class

2

FLASHLIGHT CARD
YEAR-ROUND CLASSROOM GUIDANCE GAMES
© 2007 MAR∗CO PRODUCTS, INC. 1-800-448-2197

Talking while the teacher talks

3

FLASHLIGHT CARD
YEAR-ROUND CLASSROOM GUIDANCE GAMES
© 2007 MAR∗CO PRODUCTS, INC. 1-800-448-2197

Laughing if someone falls down

4

FLASHLIGHT CARD
YEAR-ROUND CLASSROOM GUIDANCE GAMES
© 2007 MAR∗CO PRODUCTS, INC. 1-800-448-2197

Raising your hand to answer a question

5

FLASHLIGHT CARD
YEAR-ROUND CLASSROOM GUIDANCE GAMES
© 2007 MAR∗CO PRODUCTS, INC. 1-800-448-2197

Yelling out the answer

6

FLASHLIGHT CARD
YEAR-ROUND CLASSROOM GUIDANCE GAMES
© 2007 MAR∗CO PRODUCTS, INC. 1-800-448-2197

Kicking others in line

7

FLASHLIGHT CARD
YEAR-ROUND CLASSROOM GUIDANCE GAMES
© 2007 MAR∗CO PRODUCTS, INC. 1-800-448-2197

Pushing others on the playground

8

FLASHLIGHT CARD
YEAR-ROUND CLASSROOM GUIDANCE GAMES
© 2007 MAR∗CO PRODUCTS, INC. 1-800-448-2197

Throwing food on the floor in the cafeteria

9

FLASHLIGHT CARD
YEAR-ROUND CLASSROOM GUIDANCE GAMES
© 2007 MAR∗CO PRODUCTS, INC. 1-800-448-2197

Slapping someone in the face

10

FLASHLIGHT CARD
YEAR-ROUND CLASSROOM GUIDANCE GAMES
© 2007 MAR∗CO PRODUCTS, INC. 1-800-448-2197

Not listening to the teacher

11

FLASHLIGHT CARD
YEAR-ROUND CLASSROOM GUIDANCE GAMES
© 2007 MAR∗CO PRODUCTS, INC. 1-800-448-2197

Opening the door for someone whose hands are full

12

FLASHLIGHT CARD
YEAR-ROUND CLASSROOM GUIDANCE GAMES
© 2007 MAR∗CO PRODUCTS, INC. 1-800-448-2197

Smiling at others in a friendly way

13

FLASHLIGHT CARD
YEAR-ROUND CLASSROOM GUIDANCE GAMES
© 2007 MAR∗CO PRODUCTS, INC. 1-800-448-2197

Speaking nicely to others

14

FLASHLIGHT CARD
YEAR-ROUND CLASSROOM GUIDANCE GAMES
© 2007 MAR∗CO PRODUCTS, INC. 1-800-448-2197

Using good words and not bad, ugly words

15

FLASHLIGHT CARD
YEAR-ROUND CLASSROOM GUIDANCE GAMES
© 2007 MAR∗CO PRODUCTS, INC. 1-800-448-2197

Yelling nasty remarks at someone

16

FLASHLIGHT CARD
YEAR-ROUND CLASSROOM GUIDANCE GAMES
© 2007 MAR∗CO PRODUCTS, INC. 1-800-448-2197

Calling someone a bad name

17

FLASHLIGHT CARD
YEAR-ROUND CLASSROOM GUIDANCE GAMES
© 2007 MAR∗CO PRODUCTS, INC. 1-800-448-2197

Making fun of someone's mom

18

FLASHLIGHT CARD
YEAR-ROUND CLASSROOM GUIDANCE GAMES
© 2007 MAR∗CO PRODUCTS, INC. 1-800-448-2197

Laughing if someone's dad loses his job

19

FLASHLIGHT CARD
YEAR-ROUND CLASSROOM GUIDANCE GAMES
© 2007 MAR∗CO PRODUCTS, INC. 1-800-448-2197

Peeking at someone in the restroom

20

FLASHLIGHT CARD
YEAR-ROUND CLASSROOM GUIDANCE GAMES
© 2007 MAR∗CO PRODUCTS, INC. 1-800-448-2197

Running down the hall

21

FLASHLIGHT CARD
YEAR-ROUND CLASSROOM GUIDANCE GAMES
© 2007 MAR*CO PRODUCTS, INC. 1-800-448-2197

Walking down the hall

22

FLASHLIGHT CARD
YEAR-ROUND CLASSROOM GUIDANCE GAMES
© 2007 MAR*CO PRODUCTS, INC. 1-800-448-2197

Asking permission to leave the room

23

FLASHLIGHT CARD
YEAR-ROUND CLASSROOM GUIDANCE GAMES
© 2007 MAR*CO PRODUCTS, INC. 1-800-448-2197

Turning classwork in on time

24

FLASHLIGHT CARD
YEAR-ROUND CLASSROOM GUIDANCE GAMES
© 2007 MAR*CO PRODUCTS, INC. 1-800-448-2197

Taking someone's pencil without permission

25

FLASHLIGHT CARD
YEAR-ROUND CLASSROOM GUIDANCE GAMES
© 2007 MAR*CO PRODUCTS, INC. 1-800-448-2197

Asking to borrow a classmate's crayons.

26

FLASHLIGHT CARD
YEAR-ROUND CLASSROOM GUIDANCE GAMES
© 2007 MAR*CO PRODUCTS, INC. 1-800-448-2197

Laughing when a classmate doesn't know the answer to a question.

27

FLASHLIGHT CARD
YEAR-ROUND CLASSROOM GUIDANCE GAMES
© 2007 MAR*CO PRODUCTS, INC. 1-800-448-2197

Inviting a new student to eat lunch with you.

28

FLASHLIGHT CARD
YEAR-ROUND CLASSROOM GUIDANCE GAMES
© 2007 MAR*CO PRODUCTS, INC. 1-800-448-2197

Whispering to a classmate during a test.

29

FLASHLIGHT CARD
YEAR-ROUND CLASSROOM GUIDANCE GAMES
© 2007 MAR*CO PRODUCTS, INC. 1-800-448-2197

Looking only at your own paper when taking a test.

30

FLASHLIGHT CARD
YEAR-ROUND CLASSROOM GUIDANCE GAMES
© 2007 MAR*CO PRODUCTS, INC. 1-800-448-2197

RED LIGHT, GREEN LIGHT
Conflict Resolution/Martin Luther King Jr. Day/Grades 3-5

PURPOSE:

To teach students to recognize nonviolent and violent responses to situations

OBJECTIVE:

To earn points by recognizing violent and nonviolent responses

MATERIALS NEEDED:

For each student:
- ☐ Piece of paper
- ☐ Red and green crayon or marker
- ☐ Pencil

For the leader:
- ☐ Situation Cards (pages 80-82)
- ☐ Cardstock or paper
- ☐ Scissors

GAME PREPARATION:

Reproduce the Situation Cards on paper or cardstock and cut the cards apart. Laminate the cards for durability (optional). Shuffle the violent and nonviolent cards together.

PROCEDURE:

▸ Ask the students to tell the class some things they know about Dr. Martin Luther King Jr. (Won the Nobel Peace Price, led nonviolent Civil Rights demonstrations, valued nonviolence, etc.)

▸ Ask:

   What is an example of one of Dr. King's nonviolent demonstrations? (Sit ins, boycotts, walks, sit downs, etc.)

▸ Distribute a sheet of paper and a red and green crayon or marker to each student. Make sure each student has a pencil.

▸ Explain the activity:

Today we will practice situations that could be handled in a nonviolent or violent way. Our activity is called Red Light, Green Light. The Red Light stands for violent ways to respond to situations and the Green Light stands for nonviolent ways to respond to situations.

Some of the situations named on the cards in this stack have violent responses. Others have nonviolent responses. It is your job to decide which is which. I am going to give a Situation Card to each of you. When it is your turn, you will read your Situation Card aloud. As soon as you read your card, you must call out, "Red Light, Green Light." At that time, and not before, each of you must make a decision. If you feel the card describes a violent response, it is a Red Light, and you must stand at your desk. If you feel the card describes a nonviolent response, it is a Green Light, and you must raise both hands in the air. The Red Light means the violent response must stop because it is something Dr. Martin Luther King Jr. would not have found acceptable. The Green Light means the nonviolent response would have been acceptable to Dr. King.

Each of you must keep your own score. Fold your paper down the middle, matching the left side of the paper to the right side. (Pause for the students to complete the task.) *Open your paper and draw a red circle at the top on the left side of the fold. Then draw a green circle on the right side of the fold.* (Pause for the students to complete the task.) *Each time you answer a Situation Card correctly, add one point under the red or green circle. If the correct response was "Red Light," add the point under the red circle. If the correct response was "Green Light," add the point under the green circle.*

▸ Distribute the Situation Cards and begin the game. After each Situation Card is read, ask the student who read the card:

What could you have done differently in this violent situation?

or

How was this non-violent response more effective than a violent response?

▸ After each student has read his/her Situation Card, declare the student or students with the most points the winner(s).

CONCLUSION:

▸ Ask the students:

If nonviolent responses are more effective than violent responses, why is there so much violence in today's world?

If someone wants you to break a school rule, refuse because you don't want to get into trouble.

If someone knocks your books out of your hands, pick up the books and tell him/her to stop it.

Let someone who is pushing go ahead of you at the drinking fountain.

Let someone else be the first in line with his/her friend.

Turn and walk the other way if there a fight is going on.

If someone calls you a bad name, just walk away to stay out of trouble.

Let the teacher know if someone physically hurts you.

Let the teacher know if someone continually hurts your feelings.

If classmates laugh at you for not doing your homework, decide to do the homework.

If a classmate hands out papers and throws yours on the floor, pick up the paper and ask him/her to not to do it again.

Tell the truth if you did something wrong.

SITUATION CARD
YEAR-ROUND CLASSROOM GUIDANCE GAMES
© 2007 MAR•CO PRODUCTS, INC. 1-800-448-2197

If someone pushes you down, tell him/her to stop it.

SITUATION CARD
YEAR-ROUND CLASSROOM GUIDANCE GAMES
© 2007 MAR•CO PRODUCTS, INC. 1-800-448-2197

When you hear bad words at school, don't repeat them.

SITUATION CARD
YEAR-ROUND CLASSROOM GUIDANCE GAMES
© 2007 MAR•CO PRODUCTS, INC. 1-800-448-2197

Let the teacher know if someone splashes water on you in the restroom.

SITUATION CARD
YEAR-ROUND CLASSROOM GUIDANCE GAMES
© 2007 MAR•CO PRODUCTS, INC. 1-800-448-2197

Throw a ball and deliberately hit someone you don't like.

SITUATION CARD
YEAR-ROUND CLASSROOM GUIDANCE GAMES
© 2007 MAR•CO PRODUCTS, INC. 1-800-448-2197

Run in the hall and knock other kids down.

SITUATION CARD
YEAR-ROUND CLASSROOM GUIDANCE GAMES
© 2007 MAR•CO PRODUCTS, INC. 1-800-448-2197

Tattle on someone to get him/her into trouble.

SITUATION CARD
YEAR-ROUND CLASSROOM GUIDANCE GAMES
© 2007 MAR•CO PRODUCTS, INC. 1-800-448-2197

Push others so you can be at the front of the lunch line.

SITUATION CARD
YEAR-ROUND CLASSROOM GUIDANCE GAMES
© 2007 MAR•CO PRODUCTS, INC. 1-800-448-2197

Don't thank someone who helps you.

SITUATION CARD
YEAR-ROUND CLASSROOM GUIDANCE GAMES
© 2007 MAR•CO PRODUCTS, INC. 1-800-448-2197

Kick people sitting at the table with you.

SITUATION CARD
YEAR-ROUND CLASSROOM GUIDANCE GAMES
© 2007 MAR•CO PRODUCTS, INC. 1-800-448-2197

Don't help people
who need help.

SITUATION CARD
YEAR-ROUND CLASSROOM GUIDANCE GAMES
© 2007 MAR•CO PRODUCTS, INC. 1-800-448-2197

Slam the door
in others' faces.

SITUATION CARD
YEAR-ROUND CLASSROOM GUIDANCE GAMES
© 2007 MAR•CO PRODUCTS, INC. 1-800-448-2197

Yell at someone in
the Media Center.

SITUATION CARD
YEAR-ROUND CLASSROOM GUIDANCE GAMES
© 2007 MAR•CO PRODUCTS, INC. 1-800-448-2197

Irritate someone by
repeating everything
he/she says.

SITUATION CARD
YEAR-ROUND CLASSROOM GUIDANCE GAMES
© 2007 MAR•CO PRODUCTS, INC. 1-800-448-2197

When you lose a
game, yell, scream,
and punch someone
on the other team.

SITUATION CARD
YEAR-ROUND CLASSROOM GUIDANCE GAMES
© 2007 MAR•CO PRODUCTS, INC. 1-800-448-2197

Throw your books
on the floor to show
the teacher how mad
you are.

SITUATION CARD
YEAR-ROUND CLASSROOM GUIDANCE GAMES
© 2007 MAR•CO PRODUCTS, INC. 1-800-448-2197

Knock someone's
books out of his/her
hands in the hall.

SITUATION CARD
YEAR-ROUND CLASSROOM GUIDANCE GAMES
© 2007 MAR•CO PRODUCTS, INC. 1-800-448-2197

On the bus, hit
another student on
the back of the head.

SITUATION CARD
YEAR-ROUND CLASSROOM GUIDANCE GAMES
© 2007 MAR•CO PRODUCTS, INC. 1-800-448-2197

Say bad words
to others.

SITUATION CARD
YEAR-ROUND CLASSROOM GUIDANCE GAMES
© 2007 MAR•CO PRODUCTS, INC. 1-800-448-2197

Laugh at classmates
who give wrong
answers.

SITUATION CARD
YEAR-ROUND CLASSROOM GUIDANCE GAMES
© 2007 MAR•CO PRODUCTS, INC. 1-800-448-2197

SNOWBALL A FRIEND
Friendship/Winter/Grades 1-5

PURPOSE:

To give students an opportunity to practice using positive ways to keep friends and to recognize negative statements that block friendships

OBJECTIVE:

To win for your team by recognizing negative statements that block friendships and by changing the negative statements into positive statements

MATERIALS NEEDED:

For each student:
    None

For the leader:
- ☐ Friendship Statements (page 85)
- ☐ 20 cotton balls
- ☐ Masking tape
- ☐ Friendship Snowball (soft ball or sponge)

GAME PREPARATION:

Reproduce the Friendship Statements. Make 20 masking tape circles and affix one side of the tape to each cotton ball. Obtain a soft ball or a sponge.

PROCEDURE:

▸ Have the students discuss things people say or do that can end a good friendship or block one from forming. (Fussing, not sharing, not listening, not caring, telling secrets, talking behind a person's back, etc.)

▸ Explain the activity by saying:

I will divide the class into two teams. Then I will ask for one good sport from each team to come to the front of the room. Using the masking tape, each of the volunteers will stick 10 cotton balls onto his or her clothing, hair, face, or arms.

The other members of each team will then see how quickly they can remove their volunteer's cotton balls by changing negative, friendship-blocking statements into positive statements.

I will throw the Friendship Snowball toward one team. Then I will read aloud a Friendship Statement. The team member who catches the ball gets to change the Friendship Statement from a negative statement into a positive statement. For example, if the Friendship Statement says, "I don't want to play with you any more," how could you change that to a statement that would keep a friendship? ("I will play with you" or anything that would preserve the friendship.) *If the catcher successfully changes a negative, friendship-blocking statement into positive statement, he or she may remove one snowball from his or her team's volunteer.*

You may reach, stretch, or lean to catch the snowball. You may not get out of your seat to catch it. At the end of our allotted time, the winning team is the team whose volunteer has the fewest remaining snowballs.

▸ Divide the class into two teams. Select the volunteers and tell them to put the cotton balls on themselves. Begin the game and play for as long as time allows. When the allotted time has elapsed, declare a winner.

CONCLUSION:

▸ Ask the students:

What friendship-blocking statements have you heard or can you think of?

How would you feel if a friend treated you with disrespect?

FRIENDSHIP STATEMENTS

I won't play with you.

_____

I can't invite you over because you have bad manners.

_____

Let's run down the hall.

_____

Your little brother is a pest.

_____

Grades aren't important.

_____

Why do you have to study? Let's go play.

_____

Your house is a lot smaller than my house.

_____

Let's pick on the person sitting in front of us on the school bus.

_____

I like my outfit better than yours.

_____

You mom does crazy things.

_____

Let me borrow more paper.

_____

Give me some money.

_____

You don't always have
to finish your classwork.

_____

Homework is easy.
Just copy mine.

February

I Spy
Study Skills-Listening
Groundhog Day

You Gotta Have Heart
Responsible Decisions
Valentines Day

Presidents' Feud
Patriotism
Presidents Day

Bright Ideas
Responsible Decisions
Inventors Day

A special Valentine for you!

I SPY
Study Skills-Listening/Groundhog Day/Grades 1-3

PURPOSE:

To give students an opportunity to practice good listening and following directions

OBJECTIVE:

To earn the most I Spy Eye Cards by immediately using good listening skills and following directions

MATERIALS NEEDED:

For each student:
    None

For the leader:
- ☐ I Spy Eye Cards (page 91)
- ☐ Cardstock or paper
- ☐ Scissors

GAME PREPARATION:

Reproduce two or three copies of the I Spy Eye Cards on paper or cardstock and cut the cards apart. Laminate the cards for durability (optional).

PROCEDURE:

▶ Review good listening skills. Include such topics as watching the speaker, not playing with anything, not talking while the speaker is talking, following directions, doing what the teacher asks, etc.

▶ Discuss the groundhog and how this animal listens and senses what the weather will be like. Explain the belief that if the groundhog sees his shadow on February 2, there will be six more weeks of wintery days. You may want to add that in Punxsutawney, Pennsylvania, people celebrate Groundhog Day by dressing in formal clothes. When Punxsutawney Phil, the groundhog, is let out of his cage, everyone looks for his shadow.

▸ Explain the activity by saying:

The class will be divided into groups of 3-5 members each. After I assign each group a number, you will practice good listening skills and following directions by doing what I tell you to do. I will tell you to do something like wiggle, then I will call out one group's number. If every member of that group does what I have told them to do before I count to five, I will say, "I Spy" and that group will get an I Spy Eye Card.

The winning team or teams will have the most I Spy Eye Cards.

▸ Divide the students into groups and assign each group a number. Begin the game by calling out one of the action words below and the number of one group. Some of the activities may be repeated and used for more than one group. Stop after each action, wait for the students to do what you have told them to do, and award any earned I Spy Eye Card before going to the next action. (*Note:* For older students, you may combine two or three of the actions.)

Wiggle
March in Place
Clap Your Hands Three Times
Tap Your Toe Two Times
Raise Both Hands
Line up at the Door
Line up at the Window
Line up Behind Me
Line up in Front of Me
Sing "Jingle Bells"
Jump in Place Three Times
Pat Your Head
Swing Both Arms Back and Forth
Hold Hands and Make a Circle
Nod Your Head
Slap Your Right Knee With Your Right Hand
Stand on One Foot
Touch Your Toes

CONCLUSION:

▸ Ask the following questions:

What most helps you listen to directions?

What makes it harder for you to listen to directions?

EYE SPY

I SPY EYE CARD
YEAR-ROUND CLASSROOM GUIDANCE GAMES
© 2007 MAR★CO PRODUCTS, INC. 1-800-448-2197

EYE SPY

I SPY EYE CARD
YEAR-ROUND CLASSROOM GUIDANCE GAMES
© 2007 MAR★CO PRODUCTS, INC. 1-800-448-2197

EYE SPY

I SPY EYE CARD
YEAR-ROUND CLASSROOM GUIDANCE GAMES
© 2007 MAR★CO PRODUCTS, INC. 1-800-448-2197

EYE SPY

I SPY EYE CARD
YEAR-ROUND CLASSROOM GUIDANCE GAMES
© 2007 MAR★CO PRODUCTS, INC. 1-800-448-2197

EYE SPY

I SPY EYE CARD
YEAR-ROUND CLASSROOM GUIDANCE GAMES
© 2007 MAR★CO PRODUCTS, INC. 1-800-448-2197

EYE SPY

I SPY EYE CARD
YEAR-ROUND CLASSROOM GUIDANCE GAMES
© 2007 MAR★CO PRODUCTS, INC. 1-800-448-2197

EYE SPY

I SPY EYE CARD
YEAR-ROUND CLASSROOM GUIDANCE GAMES
© 2007 MAR★CO PRODUCTS, INC. 1-800-448-2197

EYE SPY

I SPY EYE CARD
YEAR-ROUND CLASSROOM GUIDANCE GAMES
© 2007 MAR★CO PRODUCTS, INC. 1-800-448-2197

EYE SPY

I SPY EYE CARD
YEAR-ROUND CLASSROOM GUIDANCE GAMES
© 2007 MAR★CO PRODUCTS, INC. 1-800-448-2197

EYE SPY

I SPY EYE CARD
YEAR-ROUND CLASSROOM GUIDANCE GAMES
© 2007 MAR★CO PRODUCTS, INC. 1-800-448-2197

YOU GOTTA HAVE HEART
Responsible Decisions/Valentines Day/Grades 1-3

PURPOSE:

To help students understand how decisions and behaviors affect others as well as themselves

OBJECTIVE:

To earn the most Heart Point Cards for your team by choosing the decision that has the most heart and considers the feelings of others

MATERIALS NEEDED:

For each student:
    None

For the leader:
☐ Heart Statements (page 94)
☐ Lion Puppet pattern (page 95-96)
☐ Heart Cards (page 97)
☐ Heart Point Cards (page 98)
☐ Pink or white cardstock or paper
☐ 2 paper lunch bags
☐ Gold paper or cardstock
☐ Scissors
☐ Glue

GAME PREPARATION:

Reproduce the Heart Cards and three copies of the Heart Point Cards on pink or white cardstock or paper. Cut the cards apart. Laminate the cards for durability (optional). Make two Lion Puppets according to the directions on page 95.

PROCEDURE:

▸ Ask the students:

   How can a person's good behavior affect someone else? (Good behavior helps a person be positive, have a good day, earn others' respect, etc.)

How can a person's bad behavior affect someone else? (Bad behavior leaves others feeling bad, distracts others from schoolwork, etc.)

▸ Explain the activity by saying:

> ***The class will be divided into two teams. I will choose one volunteer from each team to hold the paper bag Lion Puppet. I will also choose a volunteer to stand between the students holding the Lion Puppets. One puppet will peer over the right shoulder of the volunteer. The other will peer over his or her left shoulder. After each heart statement is made, I will choose two new volunteers to hold the Lion Puppets and a new volunteer to stand between them.***

> ***I will give a Heart Card to each volunteer holding a Lion Puppet. One Heart Card will have a picture of a heart. There will not be a picture on the other card. Only the student holding the puppet will know which card he or she has. The puppet with the heart card will respond with a "heart" or kind statement for the person mentioned in the Heart Statement. The other Lion Puppet will respond by saying something harsh or ugly.***

> ***I will read a Heart Statement aloud. Then I will ask what each puppet thinks about what I have read. The puppets' replies will be based on which card they are holding.***

> ***I will choose one team to respond to each puppet's response. Team members will take turns choosing which puppet has a "heart," since the Lion Puppet with the heart might change with each Heart Statement. I will then ask the other team to respond to the next Heart Statement.***

> ***I will give a Heart Point Card to each team that correctly identifies the Lion Puppet with a heart. When the allotted time has elapsed, the team with the most Heart Point Cards will be the winner.***

▸ Divide the class into two teams. Choose one volunteer from each team to manipulate the Lion Puppets and another volunteer to stand between the puppeteers.

▸ Begin the game by reading the Heart Statements, selecting a team member to answer, and distributing Heart Point Cards to those who give the correct answers.

CONCLUSION:

▸ Ask the students:

> ***What helped you recognize decisions that don't help others?***

> ***What helped you recognize decisions that help others?***

HEART STATEMENTS

Someone falls down in the lunchroom.

A classmate answers a question incorrectly in front of the entire class.

A student doesn't follow the rule about not running in the hall.

Someone decides not to help the group on a project.

Someone in the class keeps yelling out answers.

No one listens to the teacher.

A friend laughs at another friend's mom.

One classmate says another classmate is dumb.

A classmate brags that he/she got the best grade.

A new student comes into the class.

A classmate has no one to play with on the playground.

Someone says another person's art picture is ugly.

A student takes someone else's snack.

A student walks around alone on the playground instead of playing with others.

A student at the table breaks another student's pencil.

A bully keeps shoving to the front of the line and knocking others down.

A student hides a note the teacher sent home to his/her parents.

A student will not participate in class and keeps putting his/her head down on the desk.

One classmate is not invited to a birthday party to which everyone else is going.

LION PUPPET

1. Reproduce the lion parts on gold cardstock or paper.
2. Cut out the parts and glue them to a paper lunch bag as shown.

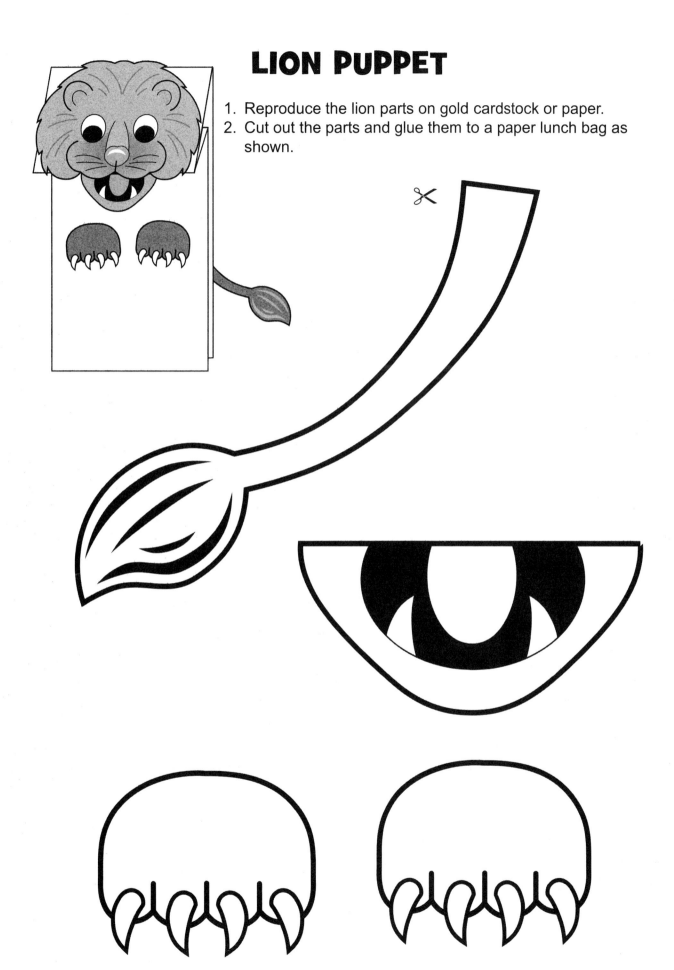

LION PUPPET

HEART CARD
YEAR-ROUND
CLASSROOM GUIDANCE GAMES
© 2007 MAR✳CO PRODUCTS, INC.

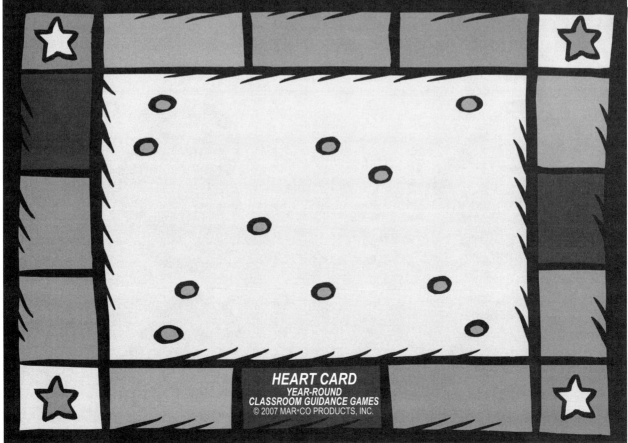

HEART CARD
YEAR-ROUND
CLASSROOM GUIDANCE GAMES
© 2007 MAR✳CO PRODUCTS, INC.

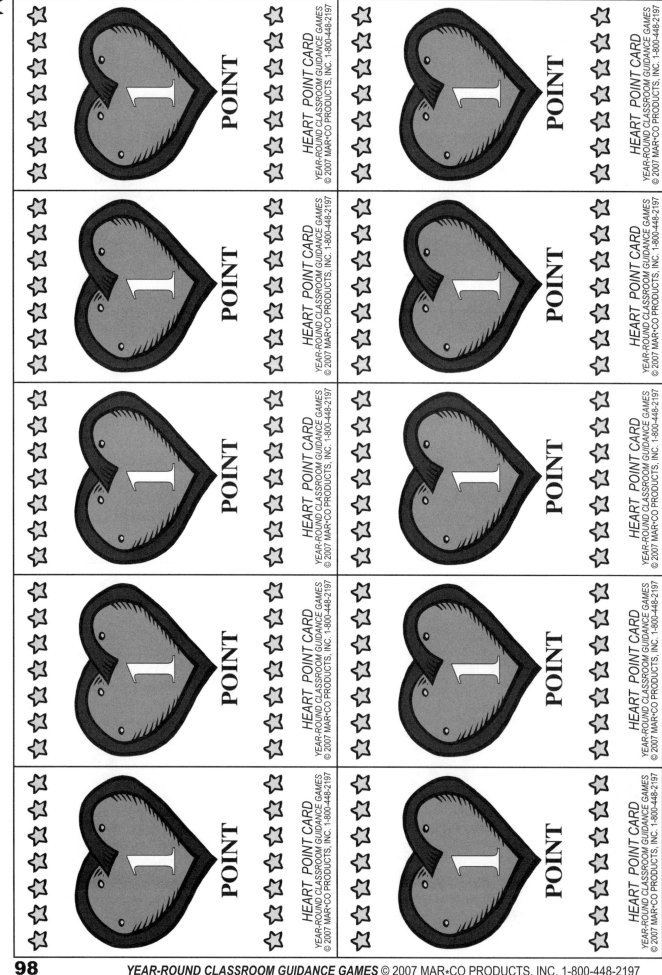

PRESIDENTS' FEUD
Patriotism/Presidents Day/Grades 3-5

PURPOSE:

To make students aware of the backgrounds and contributions of George Washington and Abraham Lincoln

OBJECTIVE:

To earn the most points for your team by knowing facts about George Washington and Abraham Lincoln

MATERIALS NEEDED:

For each student:
> None

For the leader:
- ☐ Category Cards (pages 101-103)
- ☐ Cardstock or paper
- ☐ Scissors
- ☐ Chalkboard and chalk

GAME PREPARATION:

Reproduce the Category Cards on paper or cardstock and cut the cards apart. Laminate the cards for durability (optional).

PROCEDURE:

▸ Ask the students to tell the group some things they know about George Washington. Then have them tell some things they know about Abraham Lincoln.

▸ Explain the activity by saying:

> ***Today we are going to have a Presidents' Feud. George Washington and Abraham Lincoln are the presidents involved in our feud. Our purpose is to review each man's background, attitudes, activities, and the contributions he made to our country.***

I will divide the class into groups of 4-5 members and assign each group a number. I have a lot of information about both presidents written on cards. When I read a statement, your group must decide if I am talking about George Washington or Abraham Lincoln or about both men. If your answer is correct, I will write your group's number on the board under the correct name. If the answer is correct for both names and you mention both names, I will put your group's number in both columns. When I have read all the statements, we will total the number of correct answers for each group.

Are there any questions?

▸ Make two columns on the board. Label one column *George Washington* and label the other column *Abraham Lincoln*. Divide the class into small groups and assign each group a number. Shuffle the Category Cards and begin the game. When all the Category Cards have been read or the allotted time has elapsed, declare the team with the most correct answers the winner.

CONCLUSION:

▸ Ask the students:

What new things did you learn about George Washington?

What new things did you learn about Abraham Lincoln?

How were these presidents alike?

How were these presidents different?

Died three years after leaving the office of president
—George Washington

Raised as a gentleman planter
—George Washington

Born in Virginia
—George Washington

Mother raised him
—George Washington

Lived during the Revolutionary War
—George Washington

Was a land surveyor
—George Washington

Lived at Mount Vernon
—George Washington

Lived under the Articles of Confederation
—George Washington

Married a widow
—George Washington

Didn't like political parties
—George Washington

Spoke out against restrictions imposed by England
—George Washington

CATEGORY CARD
YEAR-ROUND CLASSROOM GUIDANCE GAMES
© 2007 MAR•CO PRODUCTS, INC. 1-800-448-2197

Became president after a war
—George Washington

CATEGORY CARD
YEAR-ROUND CLASSROOM GUIDANCE GAMES
© 2007 MAR•CO PRODUCTS, INC. 1-800-448-2197

Fought in the first skirmishes of the French and Indian War.
—George Washington

CATEGORY CARD
YEAR-ROUND CLASSROOM GUIDANCE GAMES
© 2007 MAR•CO PRODUCTS, INC. 1-800-448-2197

Born in Kentucky
—Abraham Lincoln

CATEGORY CARD
YEAR-ROUND CLASSROOM GUIDANCE GAMES
© 2007 MAR•CO PRODUCTS, INC. 1-800-448-2197

Lived during the Civil War
—Abraham Lincoln

CATEGORY CARD
YEAR-ROUND CLASSROOM GUIDANCE GAMES
© 2007 MAR•CO PRODUCTS, INC. 1-800-448-2197

Led the nation as president during a war
—Abraham Lincoln

CATEGORY CARD
YEAR-ROUND CLASSROOM GUIDANCE GAMES
© 2007 MAR•CO PRODUCTS, INC. 1-800-448-2197

Became a lawyer
—Abraham Lincoln

CATEGORY CARD
YEAR-ROUND CLASSROOM GUIDANCE GAMES
© 2007 MAR•CO PRODUCTS, INC. 1-800-448-2197

Lived in a log cabin
—Abraham Lincoln

CATEGORY CARD
YEAR-ROUND CLASSROOM GUIDANCE GAMES
© 2007 MAR•CO PRODUCTS, INC. 1-800-448-2197

Wrote the Gettysburg Address
—Abraham Lincoln

CATEGORY CARD
YEAR-ROUND CLASSROOM GUIDANCE GAMES
© 2007 MAR•CO PRODUCTS, INC. 1-800-448-2197

Married and had four children
—Abraham Lincoln

CATEGORY CARD
YEAR-ROUND CLASSROOM GUIDANCE GAMES
© 2007 MAR•CO PRODUCTS, INC. 1-800-448-2197

His father was a widower
—Abraham Lincoln

CATEGORY CARD
YEAR-ROUND CLASSROOM GUIDANCE GAMES
© 2007 MAR★CO PRODUCTS, INC. 1-800-448-2197

Worked as a farmer and storekeeper
—Abraham Lincoln

CATEGORY CARD
YEAR-ROUND CLASSROOM GUIDANCE GAMES
© 2007 MAR★CO PRODUCTS, INC. 1-800-448-2197

Served as a captain during the Black Hawk Indian War
—Abraham Lincoln

CATEGORY CARD
YEAR-ROUND CLASSROOM GUIDANCE GAMES
© 2007 MAR★CO PRODUCTS, INC. 1-800-448-2197

Member of the Republican Party
—Abraham Lincoln

CATEGORY CARD
YEAR-ROUND CLASSROOM GUIDANCE GAMES
© 2007 MAR★CO PRODUCTS, INC. 1-800-448-2197

Issued the Emancipation Proclamation
—Abraham Lincoln

CATEGORY CARD
YEAR-ROUND CLASSROOM GUIDANCE GAMES
© 2007 MAR★CO PRODUCTS, INC. 1-800-448-2197

Was shot and killed while serving as president
—Abraham Lincoln

CATEGORY CARD
YEAR-ROUND CLASSROOM GUIDANCE GAMES
© 2007 MAR★CO PRODUCTS, INC. 1-800-448-2197

Raised on the frontier
—Abraham Lincoln

CATEGORY CARD
YEAR-ROUND CLASSROOM GUIDANCE GAMES
© 2007 MAR★CO PRODUCTS, INC. 1-800-448-2197

Born in February
—Both

CATEGORY CARD
YEAR-ROUND CLASSROOM GUIDANCE GAMES
© 2007 MAR★CO PRODUCTS, INC. 1-800-448-2197

Worked as a farmer
—Both

CATEGORY CARD
YEAR-ROUND CLASSROOM GUIDANCE GAMES
© 2007 MAR★CO PRODUCTS, INC. 1-800-448-2197

Ran and was reelected as president
—Both

CATEGORY CARD
YEAR-ROUND CLASSROOM GUIDANCE GAMES
© 2007 MAR★CO PRODUCTS, INC. 1-800-448-2197

BRIGHT IDEA
Responsible Decisions/Inventors Day/Grades 2-5

PURPOSE:

To make the best decision in a given situation

OBJECTIVE:

To earn the most Light Bulb Cards by correctly answering a Bright Idea Situation question

MATERIALS NEEDED:

For each student:
    None

For the leader:
   ☐ Shining Light Bulb Cards (page 107)
   ☐ Broken Bulb Cards (page 108)
   ☐ Cardstock or paper
   ☐ Scissors

GAME PREPARATION:

Reproduce two copies of the Shining Light Bulb Cards and two copies of the Broken Light Bulb Cards on paper or cardstock and cut the cards apart. Laminate the cards for durability (optional). Shuffle the cards.

PROCEDURE:

▸ Tell the students:

> *February 11 is the day that we in the United States celebrate Inventors Day. That date was chosen because it is the date that Thomas Edison, a great inventor, was born. Inventor's Day is also celebrated in countries like Argentina and Germany, but not on the same day as in the United States.*

▸ Encourage the students to name some inventors and their inventions.

- If not already mentioned, add Benjamin Franklin (bifocals), Alexander Graham Bell (telephone), Orville & Wilbur Wright (airplane), and Eli Whitney (cotton gin). For fun, you may wish to add some little-known names like Ruth Handler (Barbie Doll), Levi Strauss (blue jeans), John Harvey Kellogg (corn flakes), Walter Morrison (Frisbee), or Tim Sims (snowboard).

- Emphasize Thomas Edison's invention of the light bulb. Relate it to the concept of good decisions and poor decisions by saying:

  Making a good decision is like turning a light bulb on. When a light bulb is turned on, you see clearly. Making a good decision involves thinking clearly and considering the consequences your decision is likely to have. Making a poor decision is like trying to find your way in the darkness. You cannot see clearly. We make poor decisions when we do not think clearly or think about the consequences our decisions are likely to have.

- Explain the activity by saying:

  We are going to play a game that is like the light bulb. This game will let you see whether you can think clearly and make good decisions.

  I will divide the class into groups. Each group will have three to five members, and each member will be called to the front of the room to take a turn. Each group must decide in which order group members will come to the front of the room. When each group member comes to the front of the room, he or she will choose a card from the Light Bulb Cards. If there is a picture of a glowing light bulb on the card the group member chooses, he or she will get a chance to answer a Bright Idea Situation. If the picture on the card shows a broken light bulb, the member will return the card to the pile and return to his or her group.

  Each player answering a Bright Idea Situation must give a reasonable answer to the situation and may not use an answer another player has given. Each player who gives a reasonable, original answer keeps the Light Bulb Card and returns to his or her group.

  At the end of the game, the group with the most the Light Bulb Cards will be the winner.

- Divide the students into groups, have the groups select the order in which members will come to the front of the room. Shuffle the Light Bulb Cards and begin the game using the following Bright Idea Situations. (The situations must have varied answers and each answer must reflect a good decision.)

Bright Idea Situations:

What would you do if someone asked you to take candy from another student's backpack or a local store?

What would you say to someone who talks in a mean way to others?

What would you do if all of your friends were making fun of another student?

What would be a good decision to make if you were invited to someone's house to play?

What could you do that would help a new student?

What could you do if a classmate was being a pest while you were trying to do your work?

Give an example of a good decision you could make in school. At home. In the cafeteria. In line. On the playground. In the restroom. In the hall. In the office. When two adults are talking with each other.

Suggest something positive to say to someone who is being bossy.

▸ Begin the game and play for as long as time allows. When the allotted time has elapsed, declare the team with the most Light Bulb Cards the winner.

CONCLUSION:

▸ Ask the students:

What helps you know how to make a good decision?

What good or poor decisions have you observed?

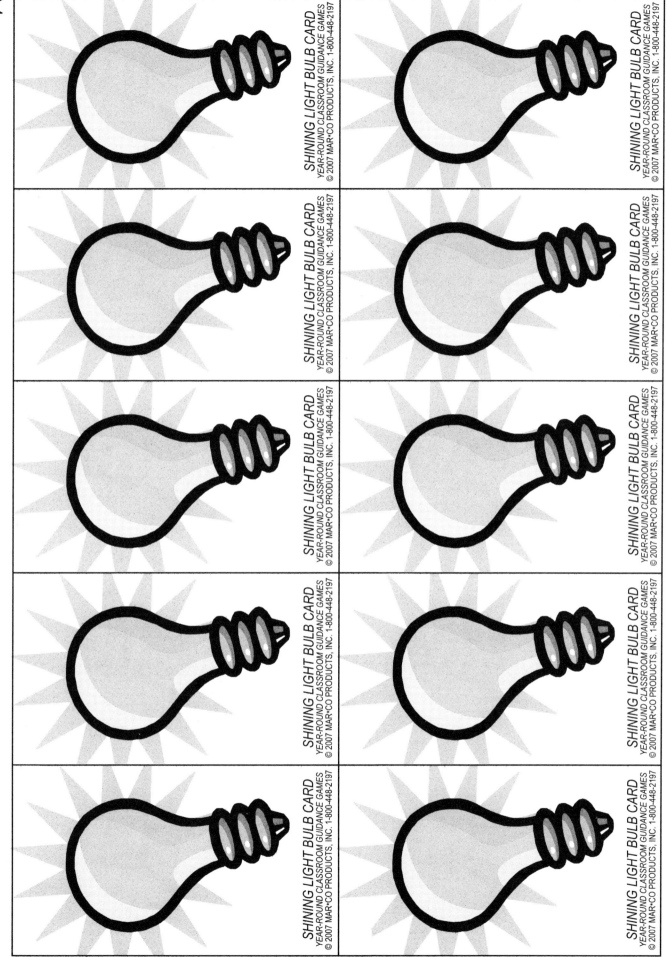

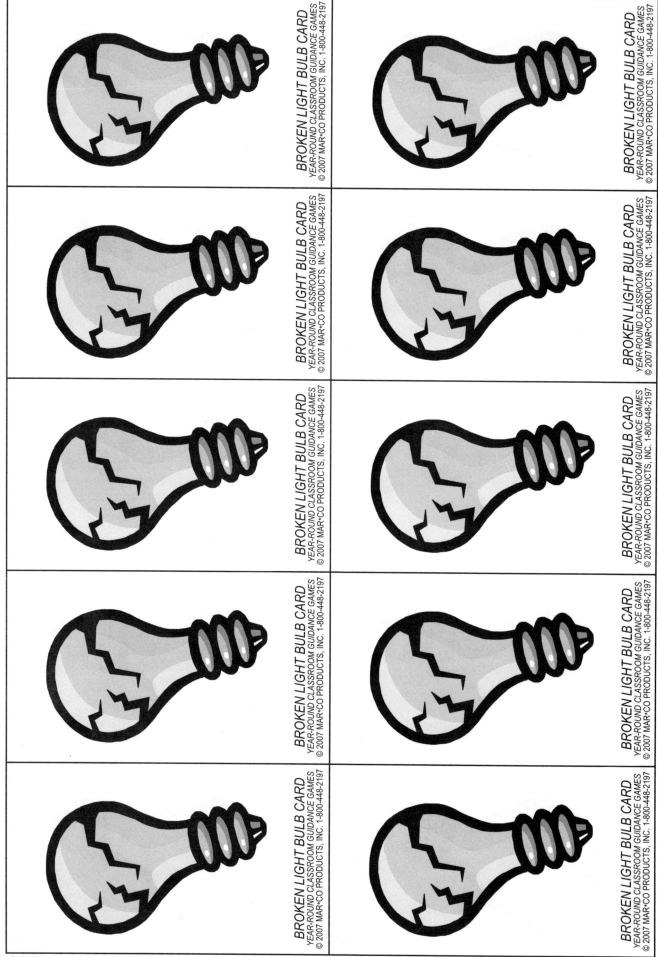

BROKEN LIGHT BULB CARD
YEAR-ROUND CLASSROOM GUIDANCE GAMES
© 2007 MAR*CO PRODUCTS, INC. 1-800-448-2197

BROKEN LIGHT BULB CARD
YEAR-ROUND CLASSROOM GUIDANCE GAMES
© 2007 MAR*CO PRODUCTS, INC. 1-800-448-2197

BROKEN LIGHT BULB CARD
YEAR-ROUND CLASSROOM GUIDANCE GAMES
© 2007 MAR*CO PRODUCTS, INC. 1-800-448-2197

BROKEN LIGHT BULB CARD
YEAR-ROUND CLASSROOM GUIDANCE GAMES
© 2007 MAR*CO PRODUCTS, INC. 1-800-448-2197

BROKEN LIGHT BULB CARD
YEAR-ROUND CLASSROOM GUIDANCE GAMES
© 2007 MAR*CO PRODUCTS, INC. 1-800-448-2197

BROKEN LIGHT BULB CARD
YEAR-ROUND CLASSROOM GUIDANCE GAMES
© 2007 MAR*CO PRODUCTS, INC. 1-800-448-2197

BROKEN LIGHT BULB CARD
YEAR-ROUND CLASSROOM GUIDANCE GAMES
© 2007 MAR*CO PRODUCTS, INC. 1-800-448-2197

BROKEN LIGHT BULB CARD
YEAR-ROUND CLASSROOM GUIDANCE GAMES
© 2007 MAR*CO PRODUCTS, INC. 1-800-448-2197

BROKEN LIGHT BULB CARD
YEAR-ROUND CLASSROOM GUIDANCE GAMES
© 2007 MAR*CO PRODUCTS, INC. 1-800-448-2197

BROKEN LIGHT BULB CARD
YEAR-ROUND CLASSROOM GUIDANCE GAMES
© 2007 MAR*CO PRODUCTS, INC. 1-800-448-2197

MARCH

If I Had A Lucky Shamrock
Friendship
St. Patrick's Day

Majesty's Manners
Social Skills
Spring

IF I HAD A LUCKY SHAMROCK
Friendship/St. Patrick's Day/Grades 1-5

PURPOSE:

To help students improve friendship skills by listening to others

OBJECTIVE:

To listen to other people, respond to the categories, and share what others have said

MATERIALS NEEDED:

For each student:
> None

For the leader:
- ☐ Shamrock (page 114)
- ☐ Scissors
- ☐ Green cardstock or heavyweight paper and a green marker
- ☐ Tape
- ☐ Glue
- ☐ 6 or 7 rulers or paint sticks
- ☐ Green glitter and ribbon (optional)

GAME PREPARATION:

Reproduce six or seven Shamrocks on green cardstock or heavyweight paper. If necessary, color the Shamrocks. Cut out the shamrocks and attach them to the rulers or paint sticks to make Lucky Shamrock Wands. Optional: Decorate the Shamrocks with green glitter and add green ribbon to the rulers or paint sticks.

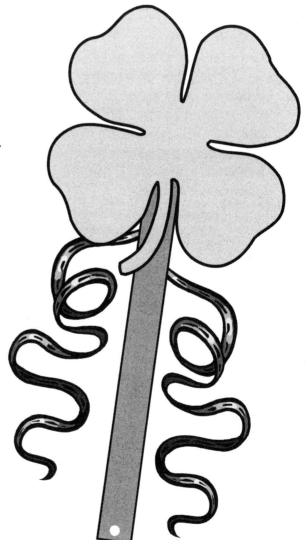

PROCEDURE:

▸ Ask the students:

> *How do you feel when friends listen to you?*
>
> *How do you feel when friends don't listen to you?*
>
> *How do you know when a friend is listening to you?* (He or she looks at you, doesn't do distracting things, knows what you have said, etc.
>
> *How can good listening help a friendship?* (It shows caring, sharing, give and take, etc.)

▸ Explain the activity by saying:

> *The class will be divided into small groups. Each group will have four to six students and they will take turns holding a Lucky Shamrock Wand.* (Hold up one of the Lucky Shamrock Wands.)
>
> *I will call out a category for the entire class to discuss within the groups. Only the person holding the Lucky Shamrock Wand may answer my question. Any other player who speaks will lose his or her turn. When the player holding the Lucky Shamrock Wand has answered my question, the wand will be passed to the player on that person's left. This will continue until every group member who has not lost a turn has had a chance to answer a question. Then I will give everyone a new category and we will continue our game.*
>
> *The categories will be similar to the following example:*
>
> > *If you could be a color, what color would you want to be? Why?*
>
> *The player holding the Lucky Shamrock Wand responds to the question, being sure to explain the reason for his/ her choice. For example, the player may say:*
>
> > *I would want to be the color yellow, because yellow makes me feel happy.*
>
> *You may not repeat a reason already given by another group member. If you cannot think of something new to say, you may ask another group member for suggestions.*

▸ Divide the students into groups. Give one member of each group a Lucky Shamrock Wand. Then begin the activity by saying:

If you could be a (<u>INSERT CATEGORY</u>) what would you be? Why?

The students will then answer by saying:

I wish I could be a _____ because _____.

(*Note:* With some groups, it may be necessary to practice this activity by having each small group come to the front of the room to answer a question. This would continue until the leader feels confident that the small groups can operate independently.)

▸ Suggested categories are:

Toy	Bird
Forest Animal	Zoo Animal
Car	Game
Pet	Food
Holiday	Movie
Flower	TV Show
Book	Instrument
Famous Person	

▸ Begin the activity and continue for as long as time allows.

CONCLUSION:

▸ Ask the students:

Was it difficult to listen to another person?

What made it easier to listen to another person?

SHAMROCK

MAJESTY'S MANNERS
Social Skills/Spring/Grades 1-5

PURPOSE:

To teach students to recognize the difference between good and poor manners

OBJECTIVE:

To wear the Majesty's Crown

MATERIALS NEEDED:

For each student:
    None

For the leader:
- ☐ Scepter (page 117)
- ☐ Majesty's Crown (page 118)
- ☐ Good & Poor Manners Statements (page 119)
- ☐ Scissors
- ☐ 2 sheets of different-colored cardstock
- ☐ Gold cardstock
- ☐ Stapler and staples
- ☐ Desk

GAME PREPARATION:

Using two different colors of cardstock, reproduce two Scepters. Cut out the Scepters and laminate them for durability. Using gold cardstock, reproduce as many Majesty's Crowns as you wish and staple them together. (*Note*: Crowns may also be purchased at a party store.) Reproduce the Good & Poor Manners Statements.

PROCEDURE:

▸ Ask the students to suggest examples of good and poor manners.

▸ Explain the activity by saying:

The purpose of today's activity is to quickly identify poor manners. The two players I choose to begin the game will come to the front of the room and stand on each side of a student desk. The players will face the desk, which will be between them.

On the desk will be two different-colored Scepters. Each of the two players will be assigned a different color Scepter, which he or she will keep as long as he or she is in the game. The players will put their hands behind their backs.

I will then read examples of either good or poor manners. Each player in the front of the room will grab his or her colored Scepter when I read an example of good manners. I will decide which of the two players grabbed his or her colored Scepter faster than the other player. The player who grabs his or her Scepter most quickly wins that round. The other player will be out of the game, and I will choose a new challenger. If a player grabs his or her scepter when I read an example of bad manners, he or she is immediately replaced with another challenger. The winner of the round will receive the Majesty's Crown to wear until another player wins. A player who wins three times in a row retires as a reigning King or Queen. I will then choose two more players to continue the game. (*Note*: If you have several Majesty's Crowns, the retiring player may wear the crown until the end of the game. If you do not have several Majesty's crowns, the crown must be given to the next winner.)

A player may grab his or her Scepter at any time during the reading of the Good And Poor Manner Statement.

▸ Put the Scepters on the desk, select the first two players, and begin the game by reading a Good And Poor Manners Statement. Read a few Good Manners Statements, then read a Poor Manners Statement. Play for as long as time allows.

CONCLUSION:

▸ Ask the students:

What helped you recognize good and poor manners?

What must you tell yourself when you see someone using poor manners?

SCEPTER

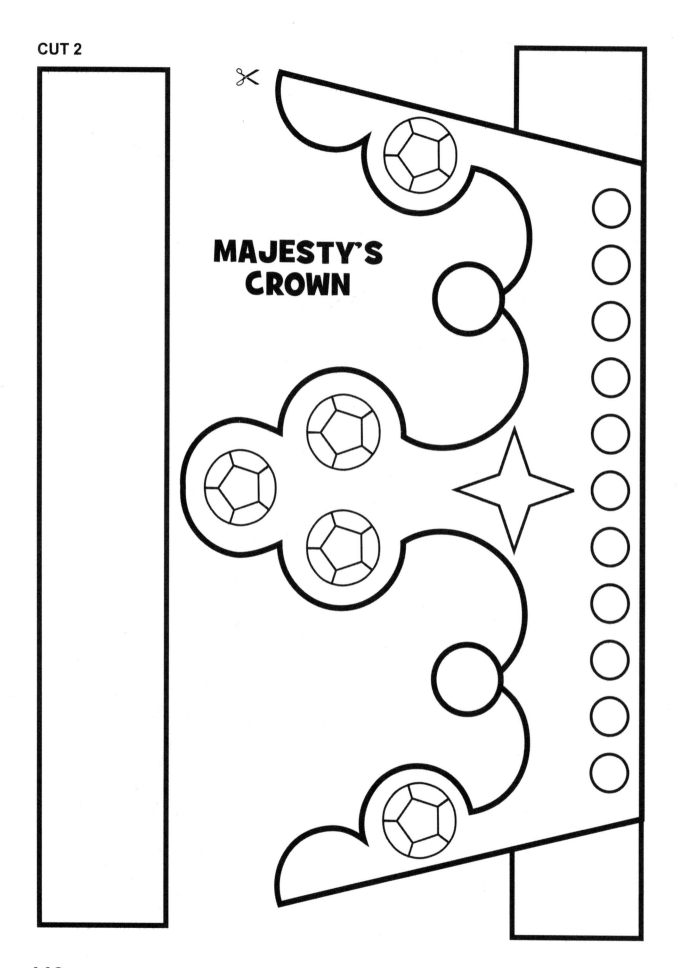

CUT 2

MAJESTY'S
CROWN

GOOD & POOR MANNERS STATEMENTS

GOOD MANNERS STATEMENTS

Waiting your turn in class
Saying "thank you" to those who help you
Smiling and looking at someone new in a friendly way
Waiting patiently in line
Staying calm if someone pushes ahead of you
Saying "hello" when introduced to someone
Helping someone who falls down
Looking at and listening to the teacher
Saying "excuse me" if you bump into someone by accident
Following the rules
Waiting until someone finishes talking to say something
Choosing words that will not hurt someone else's feelings
Letting someone get a drink before you do
Opening a door for someone else and letting him or her go ahead of you
Sitting quietly and waiting for the teacher to begin
Lending your pencil to a classmate who does not have one
Doing your best work
Walking down the hall
Walking safely so you will not harm anyone
Saying "please" when asking for something
Keeping your voice down in the cafeteria

POOR MANNERS

Laughing at someone who makes a mistake
Not waiting your turn
Pushing others
Telling friends not to play with someone else
Breaking rules
Playing with a toy instead of listening to the teacher
Not letting someone have a turn to speak
Being careless with things that could hurt others
Being selfish with materials
Making so much noise that others can't hear
Talking while the teacher is talking
Doing sloppy classwork
Grabbing things from others
Not saying "thank you"
Saying words that could hurt someone's feelings

APRIL

Bubble, Bubble
Manners
Spring

Sock-Hop-It-To-Me
Responsible Decisions
Spring

Let's Stick Together
Friendship
Spring

Bunny Hop
Social Skills
Holiday Season

BUBBLE, BUBBLE
Manners/Spring/Grades 1-5

PURPOSE:

To enable students to give examples of good and poor manners in different situations

OBJECTIVE:

To earn the most points for your team by popping bubbles and giving examples of good or poor manners for a situation

MATERIALS NEEDED:

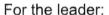

For each student:
 None

For the leader:
- ☐ Good And Poor Manners Situations (page 125)
- ☐ Bubble wand
- ☐ Bubble solution
- ☐ Chalkboard and chalk

GAME PREPARATION:

Reproduce the Good And Poor Manners Situations.

PROCEDURE:

▶ Introduce the activity by saying:

 We often hear the saying, "April showers bring May flowers." Today we are going to have a shower of bubbles. (*Note*: If you are presenting the activity in May, say a *bouquet of bubble flowers*.)

 The class will be divided into two teams. Each person on the team will have a number, starting with #1. I will invite one team at a time to come to the front of the room and form a circle.

From the team in the front of the room I will select one member to blow bubbles from the bottle of bubble solution. This member will blow one time, which could result in several bubbles being in the air at the same time. I will then call out a number. The team member who has that number will call out his or her number and try to pop one bubble. In numerical order, each team member then calls out his or her number and tries to pop one bubble. We will continue to do this as long as there are bubbles in the air. For example, if it is #1's turn, he or she calls out "one" and is the only team member who may try to pop a bubble. If #1 pops a bubble, #2 calls out "two" and tries to pop one of the remaining bubbles.

When all of the bubbles are gone, I will assign the team members a Good and Poor Manners Situation. Only the bubbles popped by team members count to earn points. Answers can be examples of good manners or poor manners. Each team member giving an example must take his or her turn in numerical order and say if it is an example of good manners or poor manners. That means if the team member who is #8 gives the first example, #9 must be next, etc. For example, a team that pops two bubbles, must give two examples of good or bad manners for the given situation. If the team members give two appropriate examples, the team earns two points. If the team members give less examples then the numbers of bubbles popped, the team receives no points. If anyone goes out of turn, his or her team will not receive any points for that round.

When all the bubbles have disappeared or been popped, the next team will repeat the process. When that team's round is over, the first team will come back to the front of the room. The first person who popped a bubble in the last round will be the bubble blower for this round.

At the end of each round, I will record the team's score on the board.

▸ Divide the students into two teams. Have the students count off. Choose one team to come to the front of the room and form a circle. Choose one student to be the bubble blower. Begin the game and play for as long as time allows. When the allotted time has elapsed, declare a winner.

CONCLUSION:

▸ Ask the students:

Was it easier to give examples of good manners or poor manners? Why?

What can happen if someone uses bad manners?

GOOD AND POOR MANNERS SITUATIONS

Someone has his/her hands full.

Your teacher is giving directions.

Your mother is on the phone.

Two teachers are talking with one another.

Someone gets sick in the restroom.

A classmate falls out of the swing.

Your parents ask you to take out the garbage.

You accidentally push someone in line.

A classmate gives the wrong answer to a teacher's question.

Your team wins.

Your team loses.

Someone says "good morning" to you in the hall of the school.

A bully picks on a small boy on the bus.

You want some candy at the store.

A speaker is presenting a program.

SOCK-HOP-IT-TO-ME
Responsible Decisions/Spring/Grades 3-5

PURPOSE:

To help students recognize negative decisions and their possible consequences

OBJECTIVE:

To earn the most socks by catching a stuffed sock and correctly answering a Sock-Hop-It-To-Me Decision.

MATERIALS NEEDED:

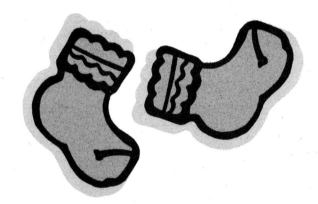

For each student:
    None

For the leader:
    ☐ Sock-Hop-It-To-Me
       Decisions List (page 128)
    ☐ Athletic Sock
    ☐ Pillow filling
    ☐ Several, old clean mismatched socks

GAME PREPARATION:

Reproduce the Sock-Hop-It-To-Me Decisions List. Stuff the athletic sock with pillow filling and knot it at the top. Gather the necessary materials.

PROCEDURE:

▸ Introduce the activity by asking:

> ***What happens to people who make poor decisions?*** (They have to accept the consequences that result from poor decisions.)

▸ Ask the group to give examples of poor decisions and possible consequences. (Running down the hall could have the consequence of knocking someone over.)

- Explain the activity by saying:

  I will begin by tossing the Sock-Hop-It stuffed sock (hold up the sock) *to someone at random.*

  The person who catches the stuffed sock gets to name a consequence to the Sock-Hop-It-To-Me-Decision I will read aloud. If necessary, that person may ask someone to help him or her respond correctly. The Sock-Hop-It-To-Me Decisions I will read are poor decisions and the player must give a possible consequence that might result from the poor decision. You must listen carefully, because if I repeat a Sock-Hop-It-To-Me Decision, the response you give must be different from the response given previously. You cannot repeat someone else's response.

  If a player names an appropriate consequence, he or she will be given a sock worth one point and a chance to throw the stuffed sock to someone else.

  If an incorrect consequence is named, I will throw the stuffed sock to another person selected at random. He or she will then respond to another Sock-Hop-It-To-Me Decision.

  At the end of the game the person with the most mismatched socks gets to hop to the front of the room in his or her stocking feet and take a bow while the rest of us applaud.

- Begin the game by throwing the stuffed sock to the first person and reading one of the Sock-Hop-It-To-Me Decisions. (*Note:* The decisions on page 128 may be used more than one time during play but must have different consequences each time.) Continue the game for as long as time allows, making sure that the students have had an equal amount of turns.

CONCLUSION:

- Ask the students:

  Are consequences necessary?

  Why is it important to think of the consequences of a decision?

SOCK-HOP-IT-TO-ME DECISIONS LIST

Kicking another student on purpose on the school bus

Yelling at another student

Telling lies about a classmate

Running down the hall

Running in the Media Center

Throwing food in the cafeteria

Pushing everyone in line

Not speaking to a new classmate who looks different

Yelling at the teacher

Not finishing homework

Not finishing classwork

Not listening to the teacher

Everyone in the cafeteria is too loud.

Everyone is too loud in the restroom.

Everyone is too loud in the hall.

Fighting on the playground

LET'S STICK TOGETHER
Friendship/Spring/Grades 2-4

PURPOSE:

To allow students to practice ways of keeping friendships by directing a friend in a positive way

OBJECTIVE:

To earn the most craft sticks by correctly answering questions about ways to preserve a friendship

MATERIALS NEEDED:

For each student:
    None

For the leader:
    ☐ Unfriendly Statements (page 132)
    ☐ 100+ craft sticks
    ☐ Glue

GAME PREPARATION:

Reproduce the Unfriendly Statements. Obtain the craft sticks.
Glue six of the craft sticks together.

PROCEDURE:

▸ Introduce the activity by asking:

   In warm weather, it's fun to eat something that will make you cool off. What are some things you can eat? (ice cream cone, water ice, popsicles, etc.)

► Then say:

Some of the things we eat are on sticks. (Hold up six craft sticks banded together.) *Would these be easy to break in half?* (No.) *Why not?* (Bound together, the sticks are too strong.)

What if I have only one stick. Could it easily be broken in half? (Yes. Break the stick in half.)

These sticks are like friends. When you have many sticks or friends, you are strong. With only one or one friend, you are not as strong. You do not have the support you need.

► Ask:

Why is it important to have and keep good friends? (Friends help you feel that you belong and keep you from being lonely, help you in times of need, can make you happy, etc.)

► Explain the activity by saying:

I will divide our class into six small groups and give each group a number. Each group will receive two craft sticks.

You are to imagine that I am a friend of yours, but I will be the kind of friend who will do or say something that could destroy our friendship. For example, I might say,

> *"I'm going to hit you if you won't share."*

I will begin with group #1 and each group member will have a chance to tell what he or she would do. The group member must not give a negative response. For example, he or she might say:

> *"If we share, we can both have fun" or "I can't play with you if you can't share."*

A group member who cannot think of a new way to respond may pass. The group will win a craft stick for each different way group members can think of to respond to the unfriendly situation.

I will then assign a different Unfriendly Statement to group #2. At the end of the game, the group with the most craft sticks will be the winner.

▸ Divide the class into six small groups and assign a number to each group. Begin the game and continue for as long as time allows, making sure each group has an equal amount of turns. When the allotted time has elapsed, declare the group with the most craft sticks the winner.

CONCLUSION:

▸ Ask the students the following:

What might have to happen if a friend continues to be unkind to you?

What qualities do you look for in a friend?

UNFRIENDLY STATEMENTS

Don't play with her; just play with me.

Let's have a club and not let anyone else join.

Your mom doesn't like me.

No one's around, so let's run down the hall.

Let's play at my house. My room's bigger than yours.

Give me some of your snack.

Your art looks messy.

Do you want some of this medicine I brought from home?
It'll make you feel really funny.

Your hair is really messy today.

Give me some of your money so I can buy an extra dessert.

I made 100 in the spelling test, and I saw that you
only made 85. I guess that means I'm smarter than you.

My brother can beat up your brother.

My clothes are nicer than your clothes.

My mom is a better cook than yours, so let's eat at my house.

I don't want to play with you any more.

I don't want to be your friend

You can't stay overnight at my house
because I have invited someone else.

I'm going to sit next to Sam instead of you.

BUNNY HOP
Social Skills/Holiday Season/Grades 3-5

PURPOSE:

To allow students to practice good manners and making good choices

OBJECTIVE:

To put the most team members on the bunny path by suggesting good manners and/or making good choices for a situation

MATERIALS NEEDED:

For each student:
    None

For the leader:
- ☐ Straight And Narrow Cards (pages 136-137)
- ☐ Cardstock or paper
- ☐ Long piece of yarn for each team
- ☐ Masking tape
- ☐ Scissors

GAME PREPARATION:

Reproduce the Straight And Narrow Cards on paper or cardstock and cut the cards apart. Laminate the cards for durability (optional). (*Note:* You may use the blank cards to write additional situations.) Cut two long pieces of yarn to make the bunny paths. Tape both ends of yarn to the floor to secure the path.

PROCEDURE:

▸ Introduce the activity by saying:

> ***Today we are going to see how many answers you can give to situations that show that you understand how to use good manners and/or make good decisions.***

‣ Explain the activity by saying:

I will divide the class into two teams and select one team to go first. Then a member of the other team will get a turn, and the teams will take turns answering a question from a Straight And Narrow Card. These questions will be about hopping on the pretend road of life and about things people do on their road of life. For example, you might be asked what you would do if you got to the drinking fountain at the same time as someone else. If the team member's answer shows good manners and/or good choices, that team member hops up the bunny path strip and waits at the end. The bunny paths are the long pieces of yarn along each side of the room.

If I decide that a team member's answer shows poor manner choices, that player returns to his or her desk (in the ditch). The team that has the most members at the end of the bunny path at the end of the game wins the game.

When it is his or her turn, a player will draw a Straight And Narrow Card. The player will give the card to me, and I will read it aloud. If the answer shows good manners and/or good choices, the player will hop to the end of the bunny path and wait there until the end of the game. Then we will count the number of players at the end of the bunny path and announce the winner. Listen carefully. If you draw a Straight And Narrow Card that was previously drawn, you must give a different answer.

‣ Divide the class into two teams. Designate each team's bunny path. Have the first player draw a Straight And Narrow Card, and begin the game. Continue the game until every student has had a turn.

Suggested answers for the Straight And Narrow Cards:

1. What would you do if your teacher gave you a note about your poor classwork to take home to your parents? (Take it to them.)

2. What would you do if you were absent from school and missed some classwork? (Make it up.)

3. What would you do with a lost kitten or dog? (Find help, but do not get near an animal you do not know.)

4. What choice would you make between working on something difficult for school or doing something easy and fun? (Do the harder project first, while you're alert.)

5. Give an example of what you would do if you saw a friend picking on another person. (Tell the friend to stop because what he/she is doing isn't right.)

6. Tell what school rule is hardest for you to follow and why it is important that you follow that rule. (Accept any appropriate answer.)

7. What would you do if a friend gave you candy that was really some type of drug? (Break off the friendship for good and tell a trusted adult what has happened.)

8. What would you say to someone who constantly makes fun of your classwork? (Stop talking to me that way or I'll have to let my parents and teacher know what you are doing.)

9. What would you do or say to a classmate who continually picks on you at school? (Ignore the person, get help, or make a joke out of it and not let him/her bother you.)

10. What would you do if someone touched you in a bad way? (Get help from a trusted adult right away.)

11. What can happen if you keep listening to inappropriate language on TV or in music lyrics? (You might begin repeating what you hear.)

12. What would you do if someone had his/her hands full? (Help him/her.)

13. What do you do and say when you are introduced to someone? (Look at him/her and give a greeting.)

14. What do you do if someone on the school bus is being too rowdy? (Get help from a trusted adult.)

15. What can you do if someone treats you with disrespect? (Tell him/her to stop.)

16. Tell us what a person should do if another student is causing problems and disrupting the class. (Tell a trusted adult.)

17. What do you do if you don't care for a certain subject? (Realize that even though you don't like it, you can't do anything about it, so it is best to just do what is expected of you.)

18. What do you need to do if you work in a class group? (Cooperate and do your share of the work.)

CONCLUSION:

▸ Ask the students:

Is it harder or easier to follow the straight and narrow road of life? Give reasons for your answer.

▸ Have the students give examples of poor manners or poor choices.

1

What would you do if your teacher gave you a note about your poor classwork to take home to your parents?

2

What would you do if you were absent from school and missed some classwork?

3

What would you do with a lost kitten or dog?

4

What choice would you make between working on something difficult for school or doing something easy and fun?

5

Give an example of what you would do if you saw a friend picking on another person.

6

Tell what school rule is hardest for you to follow and why it is important that you follow that rule.

7

What would you do if a friend gave you candy that was really some type of drug?

8

What would you say to someone who constantly makes fun of your classwork?

9

What would you do or say to a classmate who continually picks on you at school?

10

What would you do if someone touched you in a bad way?

11 What can happen if you keep listening to inappropriate language on TV or in music lyrics?

STRAIGHT AND NARROW CARD
YEAR-ROUND CLASSROOM GUIDANCE GAMES
© 2007 MAR•CO PRODUCTS, INC. 1-800-448-2197

12 What would you do if someone had his/her hands full?

STRAIGHT AND NARROW CARD
YEAR-ROUND CLASSROOM GUIDANCE GAMES
© 2007 MAR•CO PRODUCTS, INC. 1-800-448-2197

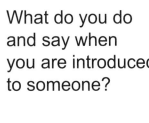

13 What do you do and say when you are introduced to someone?

STRAIGHT AND NARROW CARD
YEAR-ROUND CLASSROOM GUIDANCE GAMES
© 2007 MAR•CO PRODUCTS, INC. 1-800-448-2197

14 What do you do if someone on the school bus is being too rowdy?

STRAIGHT AND NARROW CARD
YEAR-ROUND CLASSROOM GUIDANCE GAMES
© 2007 MAR•CO PRODUCTS, INC. 1-800-448-2197

15 What can you do if someone treats you with disrespect?

STRAIGHT AND NARROW CARD
YEAR-ROUND CLASSROOM GUIDANCE GAMES
© 2007 MAR•CO PRODUCTS, INC. 1-800-448-2197

16 Tell us what a person should do if another student is causing problems and disrupting the class.

STRAIGHT AND NARROW CARD
YEAR-ROUND CLASSROOM GUIDANCE GAMES
© 2007 MAR•CO PRODUCTS, INC. 1-800-448-2197

17 What do you do if you don't care for a certain subject?

STRAIGHT AND NARROW CARD
YEAR-ROUND CLASSROOM GUIDANCE GAMES
© 2007 MAR•CO PRODUCTS, INC. 1-800-448-2197

18 What do you need to do if you work in a class group?

STRAIGHT AND NARROW CARD
YEAR-ROUND CLASSROOM GUIDANCE GAMES
© 2007 MAR•CO PRODUCTS, INC. 1-800-448-2197

19

STRAIGHT AND NARROW CARD
YEAR-ROUND CLASSROOM GUIDANCE GAMES
© 2007 MAR•CO PRODUCTS, INC. 1-800-448-2197

20

STRAIGHT AND NARROW CARD
YEAR-ROUND CLASSROOM GUIDANCE GAMES
© 2007 MAR•CO PRODUCTS, INC. 1-800-448-2197

Around–The-Character Maypole
Good Character Traits
May Day

Mother, May I?
Social Skills
Mother's Day

Pizza Party
Social Skills
End Of School Year

Missing
Good Character Traits-Remembrance & Respect
Memorial Day

AROUND-THE-CHARACTER MAYPOLE
Good Character Traits/May Day/Grades 3-5

PURPOSE:

To teach students to recognize good character traits

OBJECTIVE:

To be the last one seated after recognizing good character traits

MATERIALS NEEDED:

For each student:
    None

For the leader:
    ☐ Good Traits/Poor Traits (page 143)

GAME PREPARATION:

Reproduce a copy of Good Traits/Poor Traits.

PROCEDURE:

▸ Ask the students to name some good character traits. (Honesty, sharing, helping, caring, etc.)

▸ Ask the students for examples of poor character traits. (Lying, selfishness, not following rules, etc.)

▸ Explain the activity by saying:

> *Today we are going to have a character maypole. Do you know anything about the tradition of the maypole*? (It is a celebration of spring and usually involves skipping around a pole decorated with colorful ribbons.)
>
> *I will ask six volunteers to come to the front of the room. Five of the volunteers will bring their chairs with them and arrange the chairs in a*

circle. The seats of the chairs will face the outside of the circle as in "Musical Chairs."

The students in the front of the room will form a circle around the five chairs. They walk around the chairs, which will be our maypole, while I call out good and poor character traits. They will continue walking around the chairs as I call out traits of good character. If I call out a poor character trait, they must sit down quickly in one of the chairs. The player left without a seat will take one chair and go back and sit with the rest of the class.

We will continue our game until only one player and one seat are left. That will be the end of the round, and we will begin another round with new volunteers.

When all of the students have had a turn, the winners from each round will come to the front of the room. We will play one more round to determine the all-time winner.

▸ Begin the game by choosing the first six players. When they have put their chairs in a circle, begin naming good and poor character traits. Mention one to four positive traits before mentioning a negative trait.

CONCLUSION:

▸ Ask the students the following questions:

Can you tell us about someone you know that has good character traits?

Which character traits do you try to have? Give reasons for your answer.

GOOD TRAITS

Sharing with others
Following directions
Telling the truth
Listening to the teacher
Following rules
Using acceptable language
Being a good sport
Being friendly
Being positive
Working hard
Using good manners
Being reliable
Having self-control
Acting responsibly
Being kind
Being loving
Having patience
Being helpful
Being cooperative
Being honest
Being considerate
Being determined
Being humble or modest
Being messy
Telling in a dangerous situation

POOR TRAITS

Being selfish
Not following directions
Lying
Not listening to the teacher
Not following rules
Using foul language
Being a poor sport
Being unfriendly
Being negative
Being lazy
Using poor manners
Being unreliable
Having no self-control
Acting irresponsibility
Being mean or bullying
Being hateful
Being bossy
Making trouble
Being jealous or stubborn
Cheating
Being inconsiderate
Giving up
Being conceited
Being neat
Tattling

MOTHER, MAY I?
Social Skills/Mother's Day/Grades 1-4

PURPOSE:

To teach students to recognize good social skills

OBJECTIVE:

To be the first to reach the other side of the room and win for your team

MATERIALS NEEDED:

For each student:
　　None

For the leader:
- ☐ Mother, May I? Cards (pages 146-148)
- ☐ Cardstock or paper
- ☐ Scissors
- ☐ Chalkboard and chalk

GAME PREPARATION:

Reproduce the Mother, May I? Cards on paper or cardstock and cut the cards apart. Laminate the cards for durability (optional).

PROCEDURE:

▸ Introduce the activity by saying:

> *In this lesson, you are going to honor your mothers, guardians, grandmothers, or anyone who takes care of you. We are doing this because this person shows you about good actions in life and acceptable ways of doing things.*

▸ Then ask:

> *What are some things that this person might teach or show you?* (Good manners, good hygiene, safety issues, how to behave around others, etc.)

▸ Explain the game by saying:

Our game today is called Mother, May I? I will divide the class into five or six teams, and each team will send one member to the front of the room. It will be up to each team to decide a fair way to take turns. The members who come to the front will line up on one side of the room and face the opposite side of the room. Each player will then try to be the first person to reach the other side of the room.

Team members at the front of the room will take turns listening to my example of something a mother might teach them. If it is a good example, the person whose turn it is will say, "Mother, May I?" Then I will tell the person what movements that the Mother, May I? Card tells him or her to make. For example, the Mother, May I? Card may say: "Take three giant steps toward the other side of the room." Remember: No one may move until he or she says, "Mother, May I?" or if what I say is not a good example. If it is a poor example, the player may change the statement to a good example, then say, "Mother, May I?" If the player changes the statement to an appropriate example of good behavior, he or she may take one regular step forward.

If you move before saying, "Mother, May I?" you must sit down and another team member will take your place. The person taking your place must begin at the starting point on the side of the room.

When one player reaches the other side of the room, all the players will return to their seats. Then new players will be chosen for each team for the next round. The winning team for each round receives one point.

Are there any questions?

▸ Divide the class into teams. Select one member of each team to come to the front of the room, and begin the game. After each round, record the winning team's point on the chalkboard.

CONCLUSION:

▸ Ask the students:

Today we have been honoring mothers and other caregivers. What are some things that caregivers do for you that you didn't realize or appreciate before this participating in this activity?

How should you treat the people who take care of you?

As you eat, wipe your mouth with a napkin.

Make one baby twirl.

MOTHER, MAY I? CARD
YEAR-ROUND CLASSROOM GUIDANCE GAMES
© 2007 MAR•CO PRODUCTS, INC. 1-800-448-2197

Don't put your mouth on the water fountain while drinking.

March like a soldier six steps.

MOTHER, MAY I? CARD
YEAR-ROUND CLASSROOM GUIDANCE GAMES
© 2007 MAR•CO PRODUCTS, INC. 1-800-448-2197

Be patient while awaiting your turn in a line.

Take three stiff-legged steps.

MOTHER, MAY I? CARD
YEAR-ROUND CLASSROOM GUIDANCE GAMES
© 2007 MAR•CO PRODUCTS, INC. 1-800-448-2197

Don't talk during a show or program.

Take two sideways slides.

MOTHER, MAY I? CARD
YEAR-ROUND CLASSROOM GUIDANCE GAMES
© 2007 MAR•CO PRODUCTS, INC. 1-800-448-2197

Talk softly at the table.

Take one regular step.

MOTHER, MAY I? CARD
YEAR-ROUND CLASSROOM GUIDANCE GAMES
© 2007 MAR•CO PRODUCTS, INC. 1-800-448-2197

Look at an adult when he/she speaks to you.

Slide backward two times.

MOTHER, MAY I? CARD
YEAR-ROUND CLASSROOM GUIDANCE GAMES
© 2007 MAR•CO PRODUCTS, INC. 1-800-448-2197

Introduce people you know to new people.

Make one baby jump on two feet.

MOTHER, MAY I? CARD
YEAR-ROUND CLASSROOM GUIDANCE GAMES
© 2007 MAR•CO PRODUCTS, INC. 1-800-448-2197

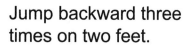

Do not laugh at someone who makes a mistake.

Jump backward three times on two feet.

MOTHER, MAY I? CARD
YEAR-ROUND CLASSROOM GUIDANCE GAMES
© 2007 MAR•CO PRODUCTS, INC. 1-800-448-2197

Help others without being asked.

Skip three times.

MOTHER, MAY I? CARD
YEAR-ROUND CLASSROOM GUIDANCE GAMES
© 2007 MAR•CO PRODUCTS, INC. 1-800-448-2197

Wash your hands before eating.

Hold your ankles and do three duck steps.

MOTHER, MAY I? CARD
YEAR-ROUND CLASSROOM GUIDANCE GAMES
© 2007 MAR•CO PRODUCTS, INC. 1-800-448-2197

Talk about good things while you eat and not about things that might make someone sick.

Take one giant skip.

MOTHER, MAY I? CARD
YEAR-ROUND CLASSROOM GUIDANCE GAMES
© 2007 MAR•CO PRODUCTS, INC. 1-800-448-2197

Sit up straight.

Take three regular-sized steps.

MOTHER, MAY I? CARD
YEAR-ROUND CLASSROOM GUIDANCE GAMES
© 2007 MAR•CO PRODUCTS, INC. 1-800-448-2197

Don't talk with food in your mouth.

Twirl forward two times.

MOTHER, MAY I? CARD
YEAR-ROUND CLASSROOM GUIDANCE GAMES
© 2007 MAR•CO PRODUCTS, INC. 1-800-448-2197

Don't interrupt adults while they're talking.

Walk backward two small steps.

MOTHER, MAY I? CARD
YEAR-ROUND CLASSROOM GUIDANCE GAMES
© 2007 MAR•CO PRODUCTS, INC. 1-800-448-2197

Listen to the teacher.

Hop on your right foot three times.

MOTHER, MAY I? CARD
YEAR-ROUND CLASSROOM GUIDANCE GAMES
© 2007 MAR•CO PRODUCTS, INC. 1-800-448-2197

Keep your clothes clean.

Take four baby steps.

MOTHER, MAY I? CARD
YEAR-ROUND CLASSROOM GUIDANCE GAMES
© 2007 MAR•CO PRODUCTS, INC. 1-800-448-2197

Use good manners on the phone.

Take one giant slide forward.

MOTHER, MAY I? CARD
YEAR-ROUND CLASSROOM GUIDANCE GAMES
© 2007 MAR•CO PRODUCTS, INC. 1-800-448-2197

Eat with your knife, fork, and spoon and not your fingers.

Tiptoe five baby steps.

MOTHER, MAY I? CARD
YEAR-ROUND CLASSROOM GUIDANCE GAMES
© 2007 MAR•CO PRODUCTS, INC. 1-800-448-2197

Don't spit your food out.

Crawl two crawls.

MOTHER, MAY I? CARD
YEAR-ROUND CLASSROOM GUIDANCE GAMES
© 2007 MAR•CO PRODUCTS, INC. 1-800-448-2197

Keep your hands and feet to yourself.

Dance forward four moves.

MOTHER, MAY I? CARD
YEAR-ROUND CLASSROOM GUIDANCE GAMES
© 2007 MAR•CO PRODUCTS, INC. 1-800-448-2197

Slump in your seat.

MOTHER, MAY I? CARD
YEAR-ROUND CLASSROOM GUIDANCE GAMES
© 2007 MAR•CO PRODUCTS, INC. 1-800-448-2197

Keep your mouth open while you eat.

MOTHER, MAY I? CARD
YEAR-ROUND CLASSROOM GUIDANCE GAMES
© 2007 MAR•CO PRODUCTS, INC. 1-800-448-2197

Throw food on the floor.

MOTHER, MAY I? CARD
YEAR-ROUND CLASSROOM GUIDANCE GAMES
© 2007 MAR•CO PRODUCTS, INC. 1-800-448-2197

Track mud all over the floor.

MOTHER, MAY I? CARD
YEAR-ROUND CLASSROOM GUIDANCE GAMES
© 2007 MAR•CO PRODUCTS, INC. 1-800-448-2197

Throw your toys all over the house.

MOTHER, MAY I? CARD
YEAR-ROUND CLASSROOM GUIDANCE GAMES
© 2007 MAR•CO PRODUCTS, INC. 1-800-448-2197

Don't pick up your clothes.

MOTHER, MAY I? CARD
YEAR-ROUND CLASSROOM GUIDANCE GAMES
© 2007 MAR•CO PRODUCTS, INC. 1-800-448-2197

Wear the same socks every day.

MOTHER, MAY I? CARD
YEAR-ROUND CLASSROOM GUIDANCE GAMES
© 2007 MAR•CO PRODUCTS, INC. 1-800-448-2197

Tear up things that belong to others.

MOTHER, MAY I? CARD
YEAR-ROUND CLASSROOM GUIDANCE GAMES
© 2007 MAR•CO PRODUCTS, INC. 1-800-448-2197

Whine about something you want.

MOTHER, MAY I? CARD
YEAR-ROUND CLASSROOM GUIDANCE GAMES
© 2007 MAR•CO PRODUCTS, INC. 1-800-448-2197

Yell out to be first.

MOTHER, MAY I? CARD
YEAR-ROUND CLASSROOM GUIDANCE GAMES
© 2007 MAR•CO PRODUCTS, INC. 1-800-448-2197

PIZZA PARTY
Social Skills/End Of School Year/Grades 2-5

PURPOSE:

To give the students an opportunity to practice good manners

OBJECTIVE:

To keep the most slices of pizza for your group

MATERIALS NEEDED:

For each student:
    None

For the leader:
    ☐ Pizza Crust (page 152)
    ☐ Pizza Toppings (page 153)
    ☐ Cardstock or heavyweight paper
    ☐ Markers
    ☐ Scissors

GAME PREPARATION:

Reproduce on cardstock or heavyweight paper enough copies of the Pizza Crust and Pizza Toppings for each group to have one of each. Use markers to color in the Pizza Toppings. Cut out the Pizza Toppings and the Pizza Crust. Cut apart the Pizza Toppings so there are eight slices for each piece of crust. Laminate the Pizza Crust and Pizza Toppings for durability.

PROCEDURE:

▸ Introduce the lesson by saying:

> *Today you will be discussing good manners. You will do this by listening to me explain different things about good manners. As you participate, you must show good manners by listening to others, respecting another's turn, raising your hands when you want to speak, contributing ideas, and being kind to others.*

▶ Explain the activity by saying:

I will divide the class into small groups. Each group will have one pizza crust and eight slices of pizza to put on top of the crust. I will choose one "server" from each small group. He or she will be assigned to another group and serve by watching that group while the discussion about good manners is going on.

I will then give the class a manners topic for discussion. When we have finished discussing the topic, each "server" will raise his or her hand to give a "tip" about whether the group he or she observed used good manners. For example, a "server" may report that he or she saw members of the group fussing, not paying attention or following directions, playing with things at their desks, bothering someone, not watching the teacher or speaker, or some other behavior that is an example of poor manners during a discussion.

I will also be watching the groups for good manners. If either the "server" or I report that a group member used poor manners during the discussion, the group will lose a slice of its pizza.

After each discussion question, "servers" will return to their groups and new "servers" will be chosen. The new "servers" will observe different groups.

At the end of our activity, the group or groups with the most slices of pizza will win the game.

▶ Divide the class into small groups of 3-5 members. Give each group one pizza crust and eight slices of pizza to put onto the pizza crust. Choose the "servers," assign them to groups, and begin with the following discussion topics:

Tell us what good manners mean to you.

Give an example of good manners in the hall; in the cafeteria; at a movie; in a program; in a classroom; when two teachers are talking; when someone has his or her hands full at a door; on the playground; on the school bus.

Tell us how you feel when someone uses good manners when speaking with you; when playing with you; when you are studying; when you are watching TV.

Tell how you feel when someone uses poor manners when speaking to you; playing with you; when you are studying, when you are watching TV.

Give an example of poor manners in the hall; in the cafeteria; at a movie; in a program; in a classroom; when two teachers are talking; when someone has his or her hands full at a door; on the playground; on the school bus.

CONCLUSION:

▸ Ask the students the following questions:

What most helps you to use good manners?

What stops you from using good manners?

PIZZA CRUST

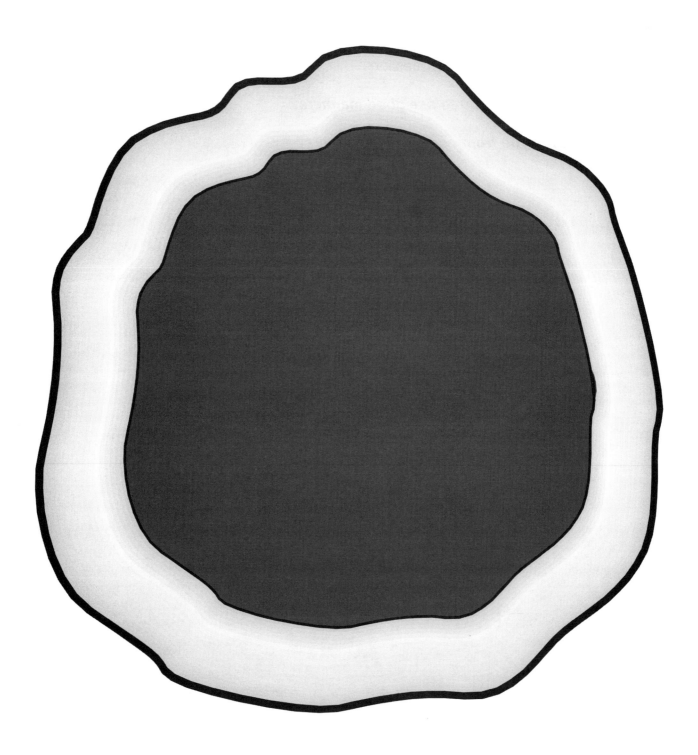

YEAR-ROUND CLASSROOM GUIDANCE GAMES © 2007 MAR★CO PRODUCTS, INC. 1-800-448-2197

PIZZA TOPPINGS

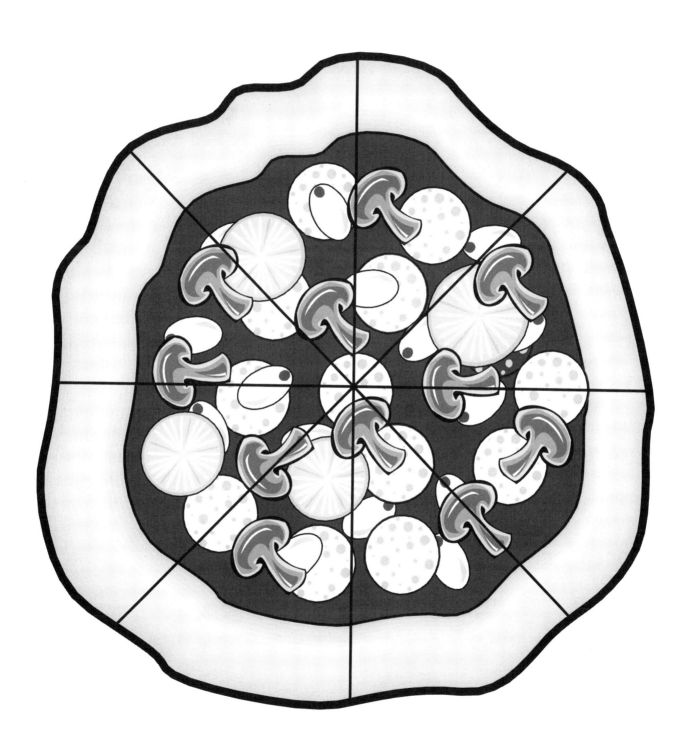

MISSING

Character Education-Respect/Memorial Day/Grades 2-5

PURPOSE:

To remember those who have died while serving our country

OBJECTIVE:

To identify an important item missing from a group of objects

MATERIALS NEEDED:

For each student:
    None

For the leader:
- ☐ 8-10 objects that are important in education such as book, pencil, paper, crayons, ruler, notebook, backpack, eraser, flashcards, etc.
- ☐ Blanket or sheet
- ☐ Table (optional)

GAME PREPARATION:

Collect the objects and place them on the table or floor.

PROCEDURE:

▸ Introduce the lesson by saying:

   Raise your hands if you have ever had a pet that died.

▸ Then ask:

   How do you remember your pet? (Look at pictures, keep toys and other things that belonged to the pet, talking about fun things you did with your pet, etc.)

   Is it important to remember your pet? (Most will agree that it is important.)

Why is it important to remember a pet that has died? (Bring out that the pet was a part of the person's life and experiences, it was loved, and it loved them, etc.)

▶ Continue the lesson by saying:

   Raise your hands if you have ever had a family member or friend who died.

▶ Then ask:

   How do you remember someone who died? (Look at pictures, look at things that belonged to that person, remember things the person said and did, learn from others about the person, etc.)

   What is it called when you remember admirable things about a person who has died? (Respect for the person because of the way he or she lived his or her life.)

▶ Continue the lesson by saying:

   Memorial Day is a time to remember men and women who have died serving our country even though we might not know these people or their families.

▶ Then ask:

   Even though we may not know these men and women, do you think we need to remember them anyway? Why or why not? (Let the students discuss their ideas to bring out the importance of how these servicemen and women have affected all of our lives by helping to keep us safer and more free.)

▶ Explain the activity by saying:

   Look at the table (floor) at the front of the room. There are eight or more items on it. (*Note:* If the items are on the floor, it would be ideal to have the students sit on the floor.) ***Each item has something to do with school and getting an education. I am going to let you come up and look at these items for a few seconds. I will then hide these objects under this blanket. After the items are all hidden, I will reach under the blanket and remove one of them. Then I will remove the blanket. It is your task to see if you can guess which object is missing.***

▶ Divide the class into small groups. One at a time, have the groups come up and look at all of the objects. When each group has seen the objects, cover the objects with the blanket.

▶ Have the students close their eyes or put their heads down on their desks. Remove one object, then have the students open their eyes or lift their heads.

- Call one group up to look at the objects and give group members one chance to guess what is missing. If they guess incorrectly, have them sit down and call another group to the front of the room. If the group members guess correctly, continue by asking:

  How is the (<u>NAME THE MISSING ITEM</u>) important in helping us in school?

  What would we do without that (<u>NAME THE MISSING ITEM</u>)?

- Replace the object. Continue the game following the directions above and playing as many rounds as time allows. Remove a different object each time and call a different group to the front of the room. (*Note*: For older students, consider removing two or three of the objects at a time.)

- Say:

  Just as each item on the table is important to us in school, each person is important to his or her family and country. Just as we had to decide what to do without the objects on the table, families have to decide what to do when they lose a beloved family member.

CONCLUSION:

- Ask the students:

  Why is it important to honor those who died in the our Armed Services?

  How are these people important to our country?

June

Home Run Choices
Responsible Decisions
Summer

Blankety Blank
Good Character
Father's Day

HOME RUN CHOICES
Responsible Decisions/Summer/Grades 2-5

PURPOSE:

To teach students to choose an appropriate decision

OBJECTIVE:

To make the most home runs for your team by choosing the most appropriate decisions

MATERIALS NEEDED:

For each student:
    None

For the leader:

    ☐ Large piece of paper or soft sponge ball
    ☐ Home Run Multiple Choice Situations (pages 161-162)
    ☐ Coin
    ☐ Chalkboard and chalk

GAME PREPARATION:

Wad the paper into a ball or obtain a soft sponge ball. Make a copy of the Home Run Multiple Choice Situations.

PROCEDURE:

▸ Discuss the meaning of *making decisions* (making choices) and appropriate and inappropriate decisions.

▸ Have the class give examples of good and poor decisions.

▸ Explain the activity by saying:

> *There will be two teams. To decide which team will go first, we will flip a coin and have one member from each team call heads or tails. The team whose member calls the coin correctly will go first.*

The first member of the beginning team will be the "batter." Before the player may bat, I will read a Home Run Multiple Choice Situation. If the "batter" answers correctly, his or her team wins a point. He or she may then bat the ball. If the answer is incorrect, the "batter" is out, the team wins no points, and the other team comes up to bat.

If the answer is correct, the "batter" throws the paper ball in front of him or herself, and hits it toward the class with the palm of his or her hand. If a team member catches the paper ball, the team will earn double points. If a player from the opposite team catches the ball, that team earns one point. This may sound easy, but you may not leave your seat to catch the ball. You may only lean, stretch your arms, or bend to catch the paper ball.

Each team that is up to bat will score one point for each correct answer, unless the batting team catches the paper ball for double points. The batting team continues until making an "out" by answering incorrectly or until three "runs" or points are made for the team. At that time, the other team comes up to bat.

Each time a team comes to bat, a new "batter" will be chosen.

The team with the most points at the end of the game will be declared the winner.

▸ Write the scoreboard on the chalkboard. Divide the class into two teams. Choose one member of each team to call heads or tails, choose the first "batter," and begin the game by reading the first Home Run Multiple Choice Situation. Continue the game for as long as time allows, repeating the situations if necessary. When the allotted time has elapsed, declare the team with the most points the winner.

CONCLUSION:

▸ Ask the students:

Which multiple choice question was easiest for you? Why?

Which multiple choice question was hardest for you? Why?

How does making appropriate decisions help you in life?

HOME RUN
MULTIPLE CHOICE SITUATIONS

(Correct answers are in boldface type.)

If someone asks you for your lunch money,
    a. give it to him or her.
    b. tell someone in authority about it.
    c. yell at him or her.

If the teacher doesn't call on you for an answer when your hand is raised,
    a. yell out the answer.
    b. tell the teacher that you were never called on.
    c. wait patiently for another chance to answer a question.

When the announcements are being made,
    a. it's time to talk.
    b. tell the teacher something.
    c. listen carefully to hear anything you need to know.

If you don't get to be the line leader,
    a. wait until next time to volunteer.
    b. whine until the teacher lets you be the line leader.
    c. push everyone to show that you don't like the new line leader.

When you're in the lunch line,
    a. take your time.
    b. know ahead of time what you want, and make your selection.
    c. yell at people to hurry up and move.

At the lunch table,
    a. save seats only for your friends.
    b. tell people to move if you don't want to sit by them.
    c. sit where there is an opening, and get acquainted with any kids you don't know.

If you don't like the lunch for the day,
    a. make a face at the lunch servers.
    b. say thank you to the servers.
    c. make bad remarks about the food to your friends.

If it's your turn to clean up in the cafeteria, *(Note*: Omit if this is not done in your school.)
    a. wipe the tables carefully.
    b. sling around the cloth for wiping the tables.
    c. yell and laugh loudly.

If someone makes fun of your grades,
    a. ignore him or her, but ask for help from the teacher.
    b. make fun of his or her grades.
    c. lose your temper or cry.

If you make a bad grade,
    a. blame the teacher.
    b. say that no one helped you understand the subject.
    c. try harder to pay attention and do your work.

If you have soccer practice,
    a. tell the teacher you didn't have time to do your homework.
    b. do your homework before going to soccer practice, by starting it in school or on the bus, or do it after practice.
    c. tell yourself that homework isn't as important as soccer.

Do your classwork because
    a. it will help you learn what you need to know for the grade.
    b. the faster you get it finished, the faster you can do something else that's more fun.
    c. you'll get into trouble if you don't.

BLANKETY-BLANK
Good Character/Father's Day/Grades 2-5

PURPOSE:

To make students aware of the responsibilities fathers have in families

OBJECTIVE:

To earn points for your team by filling in the blanks to spell words that describe fathers

MATERIALS NEEDED:

For each student:
    None

For the leader:
    ☐ Chalkboard and chalk
    ☐ Blankety-Blank Duty List (page 165)

GAME PREPARATION:

Make a copy of the Blankety-Blank Duty List.

PROCEDURE:

▸ Have the students discuss some things that fathers do to take care of their families. (Work to earn money, protect their families, watch children, repair things, etc.)

▸ Explain the activity by saying:

The class will be divided into small groups of four or five students each.

Our activity today is called Blankety-Blank because I will mark one blank line on the board for each letter in a word or words that I want you to guess. The word or words will describe something about what fathers do.

Each group will take a turn to guess a letter for the word or words that will fit on the blanks. Only one letter may be given at a time. Be careful not to

ask for the same letter another group has asked for because that will waste your turn. (*Note*: For younger students, you may want to write the letters called, but not used, on the board. Older students should have to remember the letters called. If necessary, leaders may keep a record of letters called on a sheet of paper.) *If the letter appears in the word or words, I will write it on the board*

A team will earn a point and get an extra turn for each blank it fills in. When taking the extra turn, the team may either guess another letter or guess the word or words for the blanks. If answering the word or words before all of the blanks are filled, you must call out each letter for each empty blank. If you can do this, and you spell the word correctly, your team will earn an extra 10 points.

Don't forget, if you ask for a letter that appears on several blanks, your team will earn one point for each blank that one letter fills.

If you ask for a letter that does not appear in the answer blanks, your team's turn is over. You may keep any points you have earned, but you will not earn any more points until you get another turn. Be sure to work together before deciding on a letter as a team.

Before we begin, it is important to remember that not all fathers do all the things we will mention today. The things we mention today are some things fathers can do for their families.

Are there any questions?

▸ Divide the class into small groups. Select one group to go first. Mark the blanks on the board and begin the game by using the Blankety-Blank Duty List.

CONCLUSION:

▸ Ask the students:

Which of your father's responsibilities is most important to you? Why?

Which of your father's responsibilities do you enjoy most? Why?

BLANKETY-BLANK DUTY LIST

GOES TO WORK

HAS A JOB

PAYS FOR FOOD

BUYS CLOTHES

CUTS GRASS

REPAIRS THINGS

HELPS CLEAN THE HOUSE

PLAYS GAMES

PUTS CHILDREN TO BED

EARNS MONEY

TAKES CARE OF CHILDREN

SHOPS

HELPS WITH HOMEWORK

SAVES MONEY

PLANS FOR THE FUTURE

TAKES OUR FAMILY PLACES

COACHES CHILDREN'S SPORTS TEAMS

Some Like It Hot
Anger Management
Summer

Fireworks
Anger Management
4th Of July

SOME LIKE IT HOT
Anger Management/Summer/Grades 3-5

PURPOSE:

To help students identify the negative consequences of losing your temper and practice ways to calm down

OBJECTIVE:

To practice ways of calming down and identify the best one for each student

MATERIALS NEEDED:

For each student:
    None

For the leader:
☐ Cool Down Cards (page 171-172)
☐ Cardstock or paper
☐ Scissors

GAME PREPARATION:

Reproduce the Cool Down Cards on paper or cardstock and cut the cards apart. Laminate the cards for durability (optional). (*Note:* You may use the blank cards to write additional situations.)

PROCEDURE:

▸ Tell the students:

> ***Today we will be playing a game called "Some Like It Hot." How many of you have ever felt very hot in summertime? What are some ways you can cool off when you get hot?*** (Use a fan, drink cold water, go into air conditioning, sit quietly in the shade or in a cool place, go swimming, think of cool places such as a snowy hillside, etc.)

▸ Ask for a show of hands of any student who has ever become very angry with another person.

- ▸ Say:

  This can be just like a hot summer day, when you need to cool off. It is very common for this to happen.

- ▸ Then ask:

  What can happen if you don't calm down or cool off? (Hurt yourself or others either physically or emotionally, get into trouble at school or at home, lose privileges, etc.)

  What are some ways you can cool down in a hot, angry situation? (Counting to 10, taking a walk, exercising, getting a cool drink of water, etc.)

- ▸ Explain the activity by saying:

  Today we are going to demonstrate and practice ways to cool off if we get angry about something or toward someone. It is important to keep in mind that these positive activities will not get anyone into trouble. In fact, these activities will help keep you out of trouble.

  I will ask for volunteers to come to the front of the room in groups of four to lead the group in a "cool-down" activity. One of the volunteers will take a Cool-Down Card and read it aloud to the class. The four volunteers will then lead everyone in that "cool-down" experience. Then I will ask the volunteers to suggest ways that "cool-down" technique might help them or others.

- ▸ Select the first four volunteers. Have one of the volunteers draw a Cool-Down Card, and proceed with the activity until the allotted time has elapsed.

- ▸ After each demonstration ask some of the students:

  How did this help you stay calm?

  When could this activity be helpful?

CONCLUSION:

- ▸ Ask the students:

  Which "cool-off" activity would most help you calm down in a bad situation? Why?

  Which "cool-off" activity would not help you calm down in a bad situation? Why?

If counting to 10 doesn't cool you down, try counting to 20 or higher.

COOL DOWN CARD
YEAR-ROUND CLASSROOM GUIDANCE GAMES
© 2007 MAR•CO PRODUCTS, INC. 1-800-448-2197

Count backward from 10 and try to relax with each number. Repeat this if necessary.

COOL DOWN CARD
YEAR-ROUND CLASSROOM GUIDANCE GAMES
© 2007 MAR•CO PRODUCTS, INC. 1-800-448-2197

Stiffen your arms and hands to a count of 10. Then shake them loose to a count of 10. Repeat this if necessary.

COOL DOWN CARD
YEAR-ROUND CLASSROOM GUIDANCE GAMES
© 2007 MAR•CO PRODUCTS, INC. 1-800-448-2197

Lay your head on your arms or cover your face to a count of 10. Repeat this if necessary.

COOL DOWN CARD
YEAR-ROUND CLASSROOM GUIDANCE GAMES
© 2007 MAR•CO PRODUCTS, INC. 1-800-448-2197

Run in place and work your arms back and forth for a count of 100.

COOL DOWN CARD
YEAR-ROUND CLASSROOM GUIDANCE GAMES
© 2007 MAR•CO PRODUCTS, INC. 1-800-448-2197

Sit or stand and keep your legs very stiff for a count of 10. Then shake them loose. Repeat this if necessary.

COOL DOWN CARD
YEAR-ROUND CLASSROOM GUIDANCE GAMES
© 2007 MAR•CO PRODUCTS, INC. 1-800-448-2197

Blow out all of your breath to a count of 10. Then breathe in deeply to a count of 10.

COOL DOWN CARD
YEAR-ROUND CLASSROOM GUIDANCE GAMES
© 2007 MAR•CO PRODUCTS, INC. 1-800-448-2197

Do some exercise like toe touches very rapidly. Do as many as you can.

COOL DOWN CARD
YEAR-ROUND CLASSROOM GUIDANCE GAMES
© 2007 MAR•CO PRODUCTS, INC. 1-800-448-2197

Do as many sit ups as you can. Repeat this if necessary.

COOL DOWN CARD
YEAR-ROUND CLASSROOM GUIDANCE GAMES
© 2007 MAR•CO PRODUCTS, INC. 1-800-448-2197

Shut your eyes tight to a count of 10. Repeat this if necessary.

COOL DOWN CARD
YEAR-ROUND CLASSROOM GUIDANCE GAMES
© 2007 MAR•CO PRODUCTS, INC. 1-800-448-2197

Snap your fingers as many times as you can. Repeat this if necessary.

COOL DOWN CARD
YEAR-ROUND CLASSROOM GUIDANCE GAMES
© 2007 MAR•CO PRODUCTS, INC. 1-800-448-2197

Fold your hands together. Tighten that hold for a count of 10, then shake out your hands. Repeat this if necessary.

COOL DOWN CARD
YEAR-ROUND CLASSROOM GUIDANCE GAMES
© 2007 MAR•CO PRODUCTS, INC. 1-800-448-2197

Bring your shoulders up to touch your ears and hold that position for a count of 10. Then roll your shoulders loose. Repeat.

COOL DOWN CARD
YEAR-ROUND CLASSROOM GUIDANCE GAMES
© 2007 MAR•CO PRODUCTS, INC. 1-800-448-2197

Hold your stiff arms straight out in front of you with your hands in fists for a count of 10. Then shake your arms out. Repeat.

COOL DOWN CARD
YEAR-ROUND CLASSROOM GUIDANCE GAMES
© 2007 MAR•CO PRODUCTS, INC. 1-800-448-2197

COOL DOWN CARD
YEAR-ROUND CLASSROOM GUIDANCE GAMES
© 2007 MAR•CO PRODUCTS, INC. 1-800-448-2197

COOL DOWN CARD
YEAR-ROUND CLASSROOM GUIDANCE GAMES
© 2007 MAR•CO PRODUCTS, INC. 1-800-448-2197

COOL DOWN CARD
YEAR-ROUND CLASSROOM GUIDANCE GAMES
© 2007 MAR•CO PRODUCTS, INC. 1-800-448-2197

COOL DOWN CARD
YEAR-ROUND CLASSROOM GUIDANCE GAMES
© 2007 MAR•CO PRODUCTS, INC. 1-800-448-2197

COOL DOWN CARD
YEAR-ROUND CLASSROOM GUIDANCE GAMES
© 2007 MAR•CO PRODUCTS, INC. 1-800-448-2197

COOL DOWN CARD
YEAR-ROUND CLASSROOM GUIDANCE GAMES
© 2007 MAR•CO PRODUCTS, INC. 1-800-448-2197

FIREWORKS
Anger Management/Fourth of July/Grades 3-5

PURPOSE:

To teach students to identify personal anger-provoking situations and select a way to calm down.

OBJECTIVE:

To illustrate two personal anger-provoking situations and two techniques for calming down

MATERIALS NEEDED:

For each student:
- ☐ Drawing paper
- ☐ Crayons or colored pencils

For the leader:
None

GAME PREPARATION:

Gather the necessary materials.

PROCEDURE:

▸ Begin the lesson by saying:

> *Sometimes a person can feel very angry and go off with a bang, just like a firecracker or fireworks on the Fourth of July. We know a match makes fireworks go off, but we need to know what makes you go off. What are some things that make you very angry and can make your anger explode?*
> (Not getting your own way, not wanting to do what adults want you to do, friends who do something against you, etc.)

> *What are some ways you can calm down when your anger sets you off?*
> (Counting to 10 forward and backward, holding your fists tightly at your sides, holding your breath for a count of 20 before blowing it out, taking a quick walk, etc.)

▸ Have the students practice the following ways to calm down.

    1. Move at your desk in slow motion.
    2. Stiffen your arms at your side and tighten your fists as if you are squeezing a soft ball. Do this for a count of 20. Then relax, like a wet noodle.
    3. Stiffen your legs for a count of 20, then relax them like wet noodles.
    4. Hold your shoulders up to your ears for a count of 20. Then relax like a wet noodle.

▸ Distribute drawing paper and crayons or colored pencils to each student.

▸ Explain the Fireworks activity by saying:

Fold your drawing paper in half. Now fold it in half again, then open it up. You will have four squares.

Today you are going to be cartoonists. Beginning with the first box, draw a picture of a situation that can make you very angry. You may write comments in bubbles alongside or above the characters in your cartoon.

In the next top box, draw a cartoon showing what you would like to do to calm down in the anger-provoking situation you drew in the first box.

In the two bottom boxes, do the same thing. In the third box, draw an anger-provoking situation. In the fourth box, draw what you would like to do to calm down in this situation.

You will have seven minutes to complete your drawings. When the time is up, share your cartoons with your neighbor.

CONCLUSION:

▸ Have the students share their drawings with the entire class.

MARIANNE VANDAWALKER

Marianne Vandawalker enjoyed counseling for 20 years as well as being a special reading teacher/classroom teacher for the first 20 years of her career in education. Recently retired, she is now publishing, for the next group of counselors and teachers, ideas she used in working with individual students and with large or small groups. This educator wants to share and support those hard-working individuals who guide and touch the very spirit of students in our schools.

Marianne, who lives and writes in North Carolina, is still involved in the challenging arena of education. The time she has to enjoy traveling opens up new doors for her writing.

Other published works by Marianne Vandawalker

Career Fun
Career Pay Day Game
Character Fun
Conquering Bullies
Study Skills Fun
What Could I Be?

INSTRUCTIONS FOR USING THE CD

The CD found on the inside back cover provides ADOBE® PDF files. The 10-per-page cards are designed to be printed on paper, cardstock, or Avery® #5871 white clean edge business cards. (Please note: Due to differences in the tolerances/settings of printers, the printout of the business card template version may not line up properly. If you have problems using this version, you may need to change your printer's settings. If the problem can not be resolved, please use one of the other provided pages to produce the gamecards.)

System requirements to open PDF (.pdf) files:
Adobe Reader® 5.0 or newer (compatible with Windows 2000® or newer or Mac OS 9.0® or newer).

These files offer the user color and black and white versions of the reproducible pages found in the book. For example: *016_yearroundguid.pdf* is the same as page 16 in the book.

Each PDF file may include one or more versions of the page (color, Avery® business card template, and/or grayscale/black and white versions.)

These files cannot be modified/edited.